COLERIDGE'S LATER POETRY

Samuel Taylor Coleridge

COLERIDGE'S LATER POETRY

Morton D. Paley

CLARENDON PRESS · OXFORD
1996

British Library Cataloguing in Publication Data
Data available

Library of Congress Cataloging in Publication Data
Data available

ISBN 0-19-818372-0

1 3 5 7 9 10 8 6 4 2

Typeset by Alliance Phototypesetters
Printed in Great Britain
on acid-free paper by
Biddles Ltd
Guildford & King's Lynn

In Memory of
JOSEPHINE MILES

ACKNOWLEDGEMENTS

In writing this book, I have incurred intellectual debts that are a pleasure to acknowledge. J. C. C. Mays shared with me his great knowledge of Coleridge's texts and generously allowed me to consult relevant parts of his editorial work. The manuscript benefited from criticism, both general and particular, by John Beer and by Lucy Newlyn, and Tim Fulford was a constant source of stimulating ideas. Teaching Coleridge with the fruitful collaboration of Peter Hughes at the University of Zürich greatly increased my understanding of the subject. I have also benefited from conversations with or suggestions from G. E. Bentley, Jr., Martin Butlin, Marilyn Gaull, Susan Green, Thomas McFarland, Jerome McGann, Mary Anne Perkins, Joel M. Porte, Eleanor Schaffer, Ronald and Keith Schuchard, Carl Woodring, and Jonathan Wordsworth. As ever, I could not have completed this project without the confidence and support of Gunnel Tottie.

Drafts of chapters were given as lectures at Emory University, Gettysburg College, the Wordsworth Summer Conference, and the University of Zürich, and I thank my hosts for giving me the opportunity to develop my ideas and receive comments. I am also grateful to the editors and publishers of journals in which my discussions of some of Coleridge's later poems appeared in earlier form: *The Huntington Library Quarterly*, *Studies in Romanticism*, *The Wordsworth Circle*, and *Swiss Papers in English Language and Literature*.

For permission to make use of material in collections I am grateful to the Henry W. and Albert A. Berg Collection of the New York Public Library, Astor, Lenox, and Tilden Foundations, for excerpts from Notebook Q, Notebook 29, and the 'Berg Notebook'; the British Library Board, for excerpts from Coleridge's Notebooks, other manuscripts, and marginalia as indicated in the Bibliography; Mrs Joan Coleridge and the Harry Ransom Humanities Center of the University of Texas, for lines from Sara Coleridge's Commonplace Book; the Wordsworth Trust, Dove Cottage, Grasmere, for excerpts from 'To William Wordsworth' and 'Hope and Time'; and the Pierpont Morgan Library, New York, for lines from 'To William Wordsworth' (MA 1581 [Coleridge 13]) and revisions of a printed copy of 'Love's Apparition and Evanishment' (Book No. 49359). 'The Garden of Boccaccio',

viii ACKNOWLEDGEMENTS

engraved by F. Englehart after Thomas Stothard, and Abraham
Wivell's portrait of Coleridge, engraved by W. Wagstaff, are repro-
duced by courtesy of The Huntington Library, San Marino, California,
and the the lithograph of Coleridge's 'bed-and-book-room' by George
Scharf the elder by courtesy of the Trustees of the British Museum.
Librarians and curators to whom I owe special thanks for their help are
Anthony Bliss, Frances Carey, Jeff Cowton, Mark Dimunation, Peter
Hanff, Tim Hoyer, Robert E. Parks, David Saumerez-Smith, and
Robert Woof.

With the exception of letters, most of my quotations from manu-
script sources are based on my examination of the originals, as are my
quotations from Coleridge's early editions. Texts quoted directly from
The Collected Notebooks of Samuel Taylor Coleridge, ed. by Kathleen
Coburn *et al.*, are reproduced by permission of Princeton University
Press. Quotations from *The Collected Letters of Samuel Taylor Coleridge*,
ed. E. L. Griggs, are reproduced by permission of Oxford University
Press.

M. D. Paley

Berkeley, California
April 1995

CONTENTS

LIST OF ILLUSTRATIONS

LIST OF ABBREVIATIONS

Aids to Reflection	S. T. Coleridge, *Aids to Reflection*, ed. John Beer (Princeton: Princeton University Press, 1993), *CC* 9
BL	S. T. Coleridge, *Biographia Literaria*, ed. James Engell and W. Jackson Bate (2 vols., Princeton: Princeton University Press, 1983), *CC* 7
BL	British Library
CC	*The Collected Works of Samuel Taylor Coleridge*, ed. Kathleen Coburn (Princeton: Princeton University Press, 1969–)
CL	*Collected Letters of Samuel Taylor Coleridge*, ed. Earl Leslie Griggs (6 vols., Oxford: Oxford University Press, 1956–71)
CM	S. T. Coleridge, *Marginalia*, ed. George Whalley and H. J. Jackson (3 vols., Princeton, 1980–92). *CC* 12
CN	*The Notebooks of Samuel Taylor Coleridge*, ed. Kathleen Coburn (Princeton: Princeton University Press, 1957–)
Cornell	Wordsworth Collection, Cornell University Library
CPW	*The Complete Poetical Works of Samuel Taylor Coleridge*, ed. Ernest Hartley Coleridge (2 vols., Oxford: Oxford University Press, 1912)
DCL	Dove Cottage Library, Grasmere
E	*The Complete Poetry and Prose of William Blake*, ed. David V. Erdman (rev. edn., Garden City, NY, 1982)
EHC	Ernest Hartley Coleridge
Friend	S. T. Coleridge, *The Friend*, ed. Barbara E. Rooke (2 vols., Princeton: Princeton University Press, 1969), *CC* 4
HEH	The Henry E. Huntington Library and Art Gallery
JDC	*The Poetical Works of Samuel Taylor Coleridge*, ed. James Dykes Campbell (London: Macmillan, 1893)

Lay Sermons	S. T. Coleridge, *Lay Sermons*, ed. R. J. White (Princeton, 1972)
Lectures 1795	S. T. Coleridge, *Lectures 1795: On Politics and Religion*, ed. Lewis Patton and Peter Mann (Princeton: Princeton University Press, 1971), *CC* 1
Lectures 1808–19	S. T. Coleridge, *Lectures 1808–1819: On Literature*, ed. Reginald A. Foakes (Princeton, Princeton University Press, 1987), *CC* 5
NYPL	New York Public Library
OED	*The Oxford English Dictionary, Being a Corrected Reissue . . . of 'A New English Dictionary on Historical Principles'* (12 vols., Oxford: Oxford University Press, 1970)
Philosophical Lectures	*The Philosophical Lectures of Samuel Taylor Coleridge*, ed. Kathleen Coburn (New York: Pilot Press, 1949)
PML	Pierpont Morgan Library
Poems	S. T. Coleridge, *Poems*, ed. John Beer (rev. edn., London, 1993)
SL	S. T. Coleridge, *Sibylline Leaves* (London, 1817)
Statesman's Manual	S. T. Coleridge, *The Statesman's Manual* and *Lay Sermons*, ed. R. J. White (Princeton: Princeton University Press, 1972), *CC* 6
Table Talk	S. T. Coleridge, *Table Talk*, ed. Carl Woodring (2 vols., Princeton: Princeton University Press, 1990), *CC* 14
TWC	*The Wordsworth Circle*

INTRODUCTION
COLERIDGE'S LATER POETRY

When Samuel Taylor Coleridge returned to England in the autumn of 1806, it was clear both to him and to those closest to him that his quest for health in Malta and Italy, lasting some two years, had been a failure. Dorothy Wordsworth's description of him is memorable.

His fatness has quite changed him—it is more like the flesh of a person in a dropsy than one in health; his eyes . . . are lost in it. . . . I often thought of Patty Smith's remark. It showed true feeling of the divine expression of his countenance. Alas! I never saw it, as it used to be—a shadow, a gleam there was at times, but how faint and transitory![1]

Coleridge's dependence on drugs had increased,[2] and he had produced little poetry during this period. He must have known intuitively that his most triumphant poetic accomplishments were behind him. Yet, as George Whalley has remarked on the evidence of the Notebooks, Coleridge 'did not assume that the poet was altogether dead in him'.[3] His need to write poetry remained strong. If he was to continue to do so, different modes of expression would have to be found, and forms to go with them. A 'later' poetry would not make the same claims as his greatest works, though it would frequently allude to them.

To avoid over-simplification, we must recognize that Coleridge had always had several strings to his bow, or lyre. The same three years that brought 'The Rime of the Ancient Mariner', Part I of 'Christabel', 'Frost At Midnight', 'Kubla Khan', and 'Love' also brought 'Parliamentary Oscillators', 'Fire, Famine, and Slaughter', 'Recantation: Illustrated in the Story of the Mad Ox', and 'The Devil's Thoughts' (and it might well be argued that the second group of poems was better known at that time than the first). Even his greatest accomplishments fall into widely different categories: literary adaptations of the medieval

---

[1] Ernest de Selincourt (ed.), *The Letters of William and Dorothy Wordsworth* (2nd edn., rev. by Mary Moorman) ii. *The Middle Years*, I: 1806–1811 (Oxford, Clarendon Press, 1969), 87.

[2] See Molly Lefebure, *Samuel Taylor Coleridge: A Bondage of Opium* (London: Victor Gollancz, 1974), 447–54.

[3] George Whalley, ' "Late Autumn's Amaranth": Coleridge's Late Poems,' *Transactions of the Royal Society of Canada* (4th ser.), 2 (1964), 161.

ballad form, 'A Vision in a Dream', 'conversation' poems. One of the best studies of his poetry is aptly called *The Poetic Voices of Coleridge*.[4] It is not a matter of Coleridge's previously having had one poetic voice and then finding another. Rather, Coleridge always had a number of poetic voices, but their composition and relative importance changed dramatically.

'Later' is of course a relative word. For some poets—W. B. Yeats would be a prime example—a 'later' style is the last phase in a long career marked by successive stylistic phases. For Coleridge, however, the later poetry begins relatively early. Almost all the poems by which he is known to most non-specialist readers were written before he was 30. Yet, as George Whalley has shown,[5] and as the forthcoming edition of the poetry edited by J. C. C. Mays[6] will show further, Coleridge wrote a considerable amount of poetry after that, and the last decade of his life was especially productive. It is the argument of this book that this body of work is worth serious attention.

In any consideration of Coleridge's later poetry a blocking figure will be encountered: Samuel Taylor Coleridge. The poet beclouded the critical issues by frequently disparaging his later work to others and even to himself. His motive was all too patently to avoid comparisons with his greatest poems, and his strategy took two forms: one was to lament his failing or failed creative powers, the other to classify his later productions as something other than poetry. Readers have too often taken either or both kinds of statement at face value without considering the evidence of Coleridge's deep ambivalence. For every dismissive gesture, there is somewhere a justifiable expression of pride in his later accomplishments.

As early as 1801, Coleridge was saying farewell to his career as a poet. In a letter to William Godwin dated 25 March, he provided what might be called the 'metaphysical explanation'. After telling how he had been 'chasing down metaphysical Game', Coleridge wrote:

> The Poet is dead in me—my imagination (or rather the somewhat that had been imaginative) lies, like a Cold Snuff on the circular Rim of a Brass Candlestick, without even a stink of Tallow to remind you that it was once cloathed & mitred with Flame.
>
> (*CL* vi. 714)

---

[4] Max Schulz, *The Poetic Voices of Coleridge* (Detroit: Wayne State Univ. Press, 1963).

[5] Whalley, ' "Late Autumn's Amaranth" ', 159–79.

[6] In his forthcoming edn. of the complete poetry for *The Collected Works of Samuel Taylor Coleridge*.

Where another might have used a brilliant image such as the candle mitred with flame in a poem, Coleridge employs it to support his view that he cannot write poetry, a paradox that was to be repeated.

Appropriately, Coleridge's most celebrated poetic valedictory is in poetic form, 'Dejection: An Ode', along with the verse letter to Sara Hutchinson from which it was rewritten. 'Dejection', to consider Coleridge's public statement, indeed expresses feelings of inner emptiness and of the incapacity for expression: 'A grief without a pang . . . | Which finds no natural outlet, no relief | In word, or sigh' (*CPW* i. 364). The metaphysical explanation reappears:

> For not to think of what I needs must feel,
>   But to be still and patient, all I can;
> And haply by abstruse research to steal
>   From my own nature all the natural man—
>   This was my sole resource, my only plan:
> Till that which suits a part infests the whole,
> And now is almost grown the habit of my soul.
>
> (*CPW* i. 367)

The connection between 'abstruse research' and the failure of poetic power is stated with such conviction that few have questioned it, although the 'Ode' is itself a refutation of such an argument. 'Dejection' is one of the most successful creations of a poet not unmindful of the traditional association of melancholy with the imagination. It is, furthermore, the first of a line of nineteenth and early twentieth-century poems, culminating in Paul Valéry's 'Le cimetière marin' on the theme of the inability to write poetry.

For the reading public, the 'metaphysical explanation' succeeded all too well, and Coleridge the poet was often regarded as a burnt-out case wandering in a wilderness of abstraction. These lines by Shelley, who never met Coleridge, indicate the general view:

> You will see Coleridge—he who sits obscure
> In the exceeding lustre and the pure
> Intense irradiation of a mind
> Which, with its own internal lightning blind,
> Flags wearily through darkness and despair—
> A cloud-encircled meteor of the air,
> A hooded eagle among blinking owls.—[7]

Such views were welcome to Coleridge as explanations of his failure to sustain the promise of his great early achievements. The point is not, of

---

[7] 'Letter to Maria Gisborne' (1820), 202–7. *Shelley's Poetry and Prose*, ed. Donald H. Reiman and Sharon B. Powers (New York: W. W. Norton, 1977), 318.

course, whether he sincerely believed that his imagination had become barren owing to his philosophic endeavours, for at times he obviously did and at other times he did not. We find the same discussion with others (and with himself) still going on in 1827, with the interesting difference that the metaphysical explanation is now absent. In a letter postmarked 16 May 1827, Lady Beaumont urged Coleridge to write more poetry:

Let me remind you of our last conversation wherein you said that metaphysics so far from deadening the spirit of imagination had added new wings from the power of contrast, and the last specimen you read is proof of your not having deceived yourself. Do not let the last rays sink for want of exertion, and give Fancy full play.

(*CL* vi. 731)

In the margins of this letter Coleridge wrote a response remarkable for its vehement intensity, its seemingly categoric denial, and its substratum of ambiguity:

Lady B. in this letter urges me to resume Poetry.—Alas! how can I?—Is the power extinct? No! No! As in a still Summer Noon, when the lulled Air at irregular intervals wakes up with a startled *Hush*-st, that seems to re-demand the silence which it breaks, or heaves a long profound Sigh in it's Sleep, and an Æolian Harp has been left in the chink of the not quite shut Casement—even so—how often!—scarce any week of my Life shuffles by, that does not at some moment feel the spur of the old genial impulse—even so do there fall on my inward Ear swells, and broken snatches of sweet Melody, reminding me that I still have that within me that which is both Harp and Breeze. But in the same moment awakens the sense of *C[hange] without*—Life *unendeared*. The tenderest strings no longer thrill'd.

Here is Coleridge, with no audience other than himself, using poetically charged imagery to deny his own poetic impulse. The images of the Æolian harp and the breeze that plays through it are, of course, prime Coleridgean symbols of the Imagination, going back to his first conversation-poem:

> And what if all of animated nature
> Be but organic Harps diversly fram'd,
> That tremble into thought, as o'er them sweeps
> Plastic and vast, one intellectual Breeze,
> At once the Soul of each, and God of all?[8]

---

[8] 'The Eolian Harp' (1795), ll. 46–9, *CPW* i. 102.

In 'Dejection' the harp undergoes a terrible transformation, letting out a scream of agony while the wind raves. Yet 'I still have that within me which is both Harp and Breeze'.

Coleridge's rationale—that his emotionally barren 'life *unendeared*' prevented him from writing poetry at all—is, however strongly felt, undermined by Lady Beaumont's remark about 'the last poem you read'. We can only guess at what poem that was, but it may well have been 'Youth and Age', written in the autumn of 1823, and a special favorite of Coleridge's for recitation. Among poems written between then and May 1827 were 'Work without Hope' (21 February 1825), 'The Two Founts' (spring 1826), 'The Improvisatore' (summer 1826), and 'Lines Suggested by the Last Words of Berengarius' (also summer 1826). During the months following Lady Beaumont's letter, Coleridge would write 'The Garden of Boccaccio' and most of 'Alice Du Clos', the first a poem of over one hundred lines, the second close to two hundred. Whatever his marginal note may say about his feelings, Coleridge was at that very time approaching a spurt of poetic activity.

Both publicly and privately, Coleridge felt a certain ambivalence towards his later poetry. In the strategies he adopted for categorizing this work, one senses his fear that it would be compared to the primary poems of his career. In the *Poetical Works* of 1828 and 1829 he placed almost all the poems written since *Sibylline Leaves* in a section called 'Prose in Rhyme or, Epigrams, Moralities, and Things Without a Name'. (This category was changed, one suspects by H. N. Coleridge, to 'Miscellaneous Poems' in the *Poetical Works* of 1834). In referring to such poems he sometimes used the seemingly deprecatory expression 'copy of verses', as in writing of 'The Garden of Boccaccio' to Alaric Watts: 'If you should say they are a vigorous *Copy of Verses*, you would confer all the commendation, I should be willing to receive from your Judgment' (*CL* vi. 779). 'Copy of verses', according to the *OED*, means 'a set of verses, a short composition in verse: now chiefly applied to such a composition (*esp.* Greek or Latin verses) as a school or college exercise'.[9] Yet, writing to the same correspondent, Coleridge could also refer to one or another of his recent poems as 'in sentiment and music of verse . . . equal to anything I ever wrote' and 'the flowers of my poetic life' (*CL* vi. 699); while to the editor Frederic Reynolds he wrote on 6 August 1829 that 'the Poems I had offered and read to you' [at Highgate

---

[9] *OED*, *s.v.* III. 7. I thank Professor Paul Magnusson for calling this entry to my attention. It should perhaps be noted that Alaric Watts himself used 'copy of verses' very positively in referring to a poem by Thomas Campbell that Watts had published as an editor. A. A. Watts, *Alaric Watts: A Narrative of His Life* (London: Richard Bentley and Son, 1884), i. 173.

in 1828] were 'in point of composition . . . equal to any thing, I have yet been able to produce' (*CL* vi. 805). His Notebooks and other manuscripts amply demonstrate that he considered his later poems worth the trouble of extensive revision, sometimes over a period of years. What he feared was that the reading public would think he had tried to repeat his earlier poetic successes and had—for reasons he had himself so well provided—failed to do so.

Perhaps the best way to approach Coleridge's later poetry is through the concrete instance of a poem which is in many ways typical. 'Youth and Age' was an anthology piece in the nineteenth century, 'Work without Hope' became one later, and the poems first published as 'Limbo' and 'Ne Plus Ultra' have found receptive audiences in our own time; but for heuristic purposes a more suitable example is a poem that displays many of the characteristics of the later work while, from the start, declaring its own minor nature.

'Love, Hope, and Patience in Education'

The poem known as 'Love, Hope, and Patience in Education' had its origin as a gift for Coleridge's friend, Emily Trevenen. The poet inscribed it in her album on 1 July 1829 under the title 'Reply to a Lady's Question respecting the accomplishments most desirable in an Instructress' (MS in the Cornell University Wordsworth Collection). On July 13 he sent a slightly different version of the poem to William Sotheby.[10] As the Trevenen MS is a fair copy while the one sent to Sotheby (on a separate sheet) has a number of cancelled lines and corrections that do not appear in the Trevenen MS, we may infer that the version sent to Sotheby was written earlier and revised. Some time during the summer of 1829 Coleridge supplied a copy of the poem to Frederic M. Reynolds, editor of one of the most successful literary annuals, *The Keepsake*; and it appeared in *The Keepsake* for 1830.[11] Presumably too late to be included in the *Poetical Works* of 1829, it

---

[10] *CL* vi. 798–99. The title is slightly different: 'Lines in a Lady's Album in answer to her question respecting the accomplishments most desirable in the Mistress or Governess of a Preparatory School.'

[11] Annuals collected their contributions during the summer for publication in the autumn of the year preceding their cover date. See my article 'Coleridge and the Annuals' (*Huntington Library Quarterly*, 57 [1994], 1–24), in which a number of Coleridge's other contributions to Annuals are discussed. In *The Keepsake* the title is again slightly different: 'The Poet's Answer, To a Lady's Question Respecting the Accomplishments Most Desirable in an Instructress of Children.'

appeared in that of 1834 as 'Love, Hope, and Patience in Education'.[12] In addition to standardizing the title in such a way as to expunge the poem's occasional nature and personal association, the 1834 edition alters Coleridge's typography in a way that will bear discussing.

'Love, Hope, and Patience in Education' is in several ways typical of Coleridge's later poetry. It originated as a personal gesture to a friend and was circulated in manuscript before publication. It first appeared in an annual, a mode of publication that appealed especially—though far from exclusively—to women readers. As a literary work, it relies chiefly upon the trope of personification, extending it so far as to constitute a little allegorical drama. Its rhythms are fairly regular but not mechanically so, with enjambement working to offset any tendency toward a sing-song quality. The poet's presence is felt throughout, his tone carefully modulated in the manuscript versions by the discreet use of italics and exclamation points. As the Sotheby MS in particular shows, Coleridge took a great deal of care in revision to bring the poem to a form that satisfied him.

The poem begins with the three personifications that will appear throughout—Love, Hope, and Patience—or, rather, LOVE, HOPE, and PATIENCE, for so both manuscripts read, as does *The Keepsake*. That this matter of small capitals was important to Coleridge is demonstrated by a letter he wrote to Thomas Pringle, the friendliest and most sympathetic editor of his later years, about 'Love's Apparition and Evanishment' (1833; see Ch. 4). In August 1833, after the poet received the proofs for that poem, which was about to appear in Pringle's annual, *Friendship's Offering*, he wrote:

I sadly quarrel with our modern Printers for their levelling spirit of antipathy to all initial Capitals, thus ruin'd well for ruin'd Well. I greatly approve of the German Rule of distinguishing all Noun-Substantives by a Capital: & at least, all *Personifications* shall be small Capitals: see—HOPE—

(*CL* vi. 955)

Pringle complied, and the poem was reset according to the poet's wishes, only to be subjected to the levelling spirit again when its small capitals were removed in the *Poetical Works* of 1834, as were those of 'LOVE', 'HOPE', and 'PATIENCE'. In Coleridge's mind the small capitals marked off the personifications from other noun-substantives by recognizing their special, fictive nature. This made them textually self-conscious players of parts and at the same time placed them in a

[12] As pointed out in *JDC* 644, this poem was printed on a leaf at the end of vol. iii of the 1834 *Poetical Works* and 'may easily be overlooked there'.

deliberately miniaturized relation to the concepts usually represented by such abstractions. Tilottama Rajan has termed such figures and the type of poem in which they appear 'abjects', remarking that Coleridge, 'disgarding himself from a High Romanticism which he himself contributed to constructing . . . offers his late poems as textual abjects which call into question the ideology of aesthetic form'.[13] Such a genre, like all others, establishes its own frame of reference, one aspect of which is indicated typographically. One may decide one doesn't like what such poems are trying to do, but it is important to recognize that they are not trying to do something else.

Throughout this particular poem there is a fundamental contrast (tension would be too strong a word) between the formal quality of the three figures and, especially in the texts preceding that of 1834, the conversational tone in which they are presented. LOVE, HOPE, and PATIENCE suggest a sculptured group. Collectively troped to Atlas holding up 'Heaven's starry globe', they appear in a memorable image:

> The straiten'd Arms uprais'd, the Palms aslope,
> And Robes that touching, as adown they flow
> Distinctly blend, like snow emboss'd on snow.[14]

The effect of three-dimensionality is increased by the word 'emboss'd', with its suggestion of depth. There follows a little drama in which HOPE is imagined as lying prostrate and LOVE as sinking and dying. Unlike some other late poems, especially 'Love's Apparition and Evanishment', in which such a situation has a tragic outcome, here LOVE succours HOPE with a maternal gesture, 'bending o'er, with soul-transfusing eyes | And the low murmurs of the Mother Dove'. Yet LOVE herself is not ultimately strong enough to bear the load:

> Then with a Statue's smile, a Statue's strength
> Stands the mute sister PATIENCE nothing loth,
> And both supporting does the work of both!

The sculptural quality of the imagery, only suggested before, is now made explicit in an echo of Shakespeare's 'Patience on a monument, | Smiling at Grief',[15] transformed for Coleridge's purposes. This

---

[13] 'Coleridge, Wordsworth, and the Textual Abject', *TWC* 24 (1993), 63.

[14] All quotations from the printed text refer to *The Keepsake* for 1830, 279, with significant differences between this and other texts noted where appropriate.

[15] *Twelfth Night*, ed. E. J. M. Lothian & T. W. Craik (London, Arden Shakespeare, 1975), III. iv. 115–16. On pictorial representations of Patience on a monument, see William S. Hecksher's essay, 'Shakespeare and the Visual Arts', *Research Opportunities in Renaissance Drama: The Report of the Modern Language Association Seminar*, ed. S. Schoenbaum, 13–14 (1970–1), 35–56.

imagery was once carried further to include a tribute to the contemporary sculptor Francis Chantrey; and Coleridge's decision not to use the additional material provides an illustration of his working methods to which we will return.

Evidence of the minute care that Coleridge took with this poem can be seen in his revisions, his rhythms, and his modulations of tone by means of typography and punctuation. In line 9 the original reading was 'triune group'; probably to avoid an awkward confluence of sounds, Coleridge considered 'living group', but no doubt because this would have run counter to the sculptural quality of the image he wanted to establish, this too was rejected for 'group'd in seemly shew'. 'Robe touching Robe beneath, and blending as they flow!' gave way to 'Robes that touching, as adown they flow', with its suggestion of 'down' as a noun reinforcing the sense of whiteness. Enjambement creates a sense of flow in a number of transitions, as from lines 5 to 6 and 6 to 7: 'places | Heaven's starry globe' and 'so | Do these bear up'; and the chiasmus of line 20—'thus LOVE repays to HOPE what HOPE first gave to LOVE'— nicely replicates the combination of symmetry and interaction being described. In the manuscript the underlining of 'thy' in line 3 and 'keep school' in line 4 (as also in *The Keepsake*), together with the exclamation marks that end lines 4 and 20, give rise to tonal variations and emphases that are lost in the 1834 text, weakening the conversational quality of the previous versions.[16]

Coleridge's attention to this poem in revision also extended to larger matters of aesthetic principle. In the manuscript sent to William Sotheby, the poet put an asterisk after 'strength' and noted:

In the first copy the Lines stood thus:

> 'Then like a Statue, with a Statue's Strength,
> 'And with a Smile, the Sister-Fay of those
>   'Who meet at Evening's Close
>   'To teach our Grief repose
> 'Their freshly-gather'd Store of Moonbeams wreathe
> 'On Marble Lips, a CHANTRY has made breathe,
> 'Stands the mute' &c—

This allusion to the work of a well-known living sculptor would have strengthened the imagery for Coleridge's reader, and his reason for eliminating the lines is extremely interesting. 'They were struck out by the Author,' Coleridge explained,

---

[16] Refs. to the Trevenen Manuscript are by courtesy of the Cornell University Library, Wordsworth Collection.

not because he thought them bad lines in themselves (quamvis Della Cruscam fortasse paullulò nimis redolere videantur) but because they diverted and retarded the stream of the Thought and injured the Organic Unity of the Composition. Più NEL UNO is Francesco de Salez' brief and happy definition of the Beautiful: and the shorter the poem, the more indispensable is it, that the Più should not overlay the Uno, that the unity should be *evident*. But to sacrifice the *gratification*, the sting of *pleasure*, from a fine *passage* to the *satisfaction*, the sense of *Complacency* arising from the contemplation of a symmetrical *Whole*, is among the last Conquests achieved by men of genial powers.[17]

The doctrine of 'il più nell' uno'—or 'Multëity in Unity', as Coleridge phrased it in 'The Principles of Genial Criticism', was one which he frequently restated as one of the most important in art.[18] Here we see him applying it to a minor poem with the same sense of critical discrimination that he brought to his more ambitious creations.

'Love, Hope, and Patience in Education' *is* a minor poem, and it should not be judged as a failed major one. An instructive comparison can be made with Keats's 'Ode on Indolence' (a poem not published during Coleridge's lifetime), which also features three female personifications. In Keats's ode the poet sees them while in a half-dreaming state. A sense of mystery exists until they are revealed to be Love, Ambition, and Poesy; but even after that the focus of the poem is not on them but on the poet's inner being, and the last two stanzas unfold after they are gone. Coleridge, in contrast, states immediately who his personifications are, and his poem belongs to them as they enact their assigned parts. They less resemble Keats's shadowy self-projections than they do the fixed allegorical personifications of Giovanni Battista Guarini's 'Faith, Hope, and Charity', translated by Coleridge earlier.[19] Set off from the living world by their identifying small capitals and their sculptured images, they call attention to their fictitious quality. Personification is seldom encountered in modern poetry, and even critics sympathetic to the later Coleridge have had difficulty with them.[20] Yet

[17] *CL* vi. 799 n. 'Although they might seem too redolent of Della Crusca.'
[18] See J. Shawcross (ed.), *Biographia Literaria*, ii. (Oxford, 1907, rev. 1954), 232. R. A. Foakes calls attention to this parallel in a note to Coleridge's expression 'the many seen as one' in the 1818 'Lectures on European Literature' (*Lectures 1808–19* ii. 220 n.). In *Table Talk* for 27 December 1831 (*TT* i. 261), Coleridge expatiates on the principle of '*il più nell' uno*', and Carl Woodring's note gives many examples of the recurrence of both the phrase and the idea in Coleridge's writings.
[19] *CPW* i. 427–8. Ernest Hartley Coleridge dates this transl. 1815; John Beer, in *Poems* (rev. edn., London, 1993), 430, at 1812 or 1815.
[20] e.g. John L. Mahoney speaks of the 'lackluster didacticism of *Love, Hope, and Patience in Education* with its distrust of the joys of spontaneity and its presentation of a new and stiffly personified heroine of comfort.' ' "We Must Away": Tragedy and Imagination in Coleridge's

prosopopoeia is the dominant trope of this part of Coleridge's poetic career. It may even be said that he thought in personifications, as when he wrote to his son Derwent of 'the spice-islands of Youth and Hope, the two realities of this Phantom World' and added, 'I did not add Love: for this is only Youth and Hope embracing and so seen as *one*'.[21] The role of personification is best further discussed with respect to particular poems, beginning with the one that both announces and enacts the transition to Coleridge's later poetry—the poem now known as 'To William Wordsworth'.

Later Poems', in *Coleridge, Keats, and the Imagination: Romanticism and Adam's Dream, Essays in Honor of Walter Jackson Bate*, ed. J. Robert Barth, SJ, and John L. Mahoney (Columbia, Mo.; Univ. of Missouri Press, 1990), 121.

[21] *CL* vi. 705, conjecturally dated Oct. 1807 by Griggs, who also notes the repetition of these words in *Table Talk* for 10 July 1834 (ii. 296).

'To William Wordsworth'

In the winter of 1806–7 there gathered at Coleorton, Sir George Beaumont's estate in Leicestershire, a group of intimately connected people: William, Mary, and Dorothy Wordsworth, Sara Hutchinson, and Samuel Taylor Coleridge and his son Hartley. There, over a period of several evenings, William Wordsworth read to the others his great work addressed to Coleridge, later known as *The Prelude*. It was a momentous occasion, and in commemoration of it Coleridge wrote a poem that with its original title precisely places the event:

To William Wordsworth: Lines composed, for the greater part on the Night, on which he finished his recitation of his Poem (in thirteen Books) concerning the growth and history of his own mind. Janry., 1807. Coleorton, near Ashby de la Zouch.[1]

This ambitious celebration of Wordsworth's achievement also marks an important phase in Coleridge's own history as a poet, for it renounces the grand poetry of public statement that had been so important to him from the late 1780s onwards. By representing himself as dead and in his coffin, Coleridge seems to represent the end of his poetic career while actually, as we shall see, leaving open the possibility of its rebirth in another form. 'To William Wordsworth' is thus a door that closes in one direction to open in another.

As the poem exists in two basically different forms (with some minor variations within each), we must begin with a brief account of its textual history. After writing his draft—a manuscript which he must have retained, but which is not now known to exist—Coleridge made a fair copy. This manuscript, now in the Dove Cottage Library, was presumably given by Coleridge to Wordsworth. A copy of it, now in the Pierpont Morgan Library, was made by Sara Hutchinson for Coleridge to keep. These two texts are very similar, with a few significant variants that merit discussion.[2] When the poem appeared in print in *Sibylline*

---

[1] From the DCL: see n. 2.

[2] The DCL ms was first published in *CPW* i. 579–82. Sara Hutchinson's transcript (with a few additions by Coleridge) is now with the Beaumont Papers in the PML. It was published

Leaves (1817), however, it was in significantly different form, beginning with the title, which now read 'To a Gentleman. *Composed on the night after his recitation of a Poem on the Growth of an Individual Mind.*' The three subsequent lifetime publications, in the *Poetical Works* of 1828, 1829, and 1834 vary little from the *Sibylline Leaves* version. This division of 'To William Wordsworth' into two basic versions was a result of Wordsworth's opposition to having it published at all.

In 1811, when Lady Beaumont learned from the advertisement to Coleridge's forthcoming lectures on Shakespeare and Milton that he also intended to discuss contemporary poets, she feared that Wordsworth's poetry might be attacked (*CL* iii. 343 and n.). To allay her anxiety, Coleridge sent her Sara Hutchinson's transcript. 'I sent her Ladyship the verses composed after your recitation of the great poem at Cole-orton,' he wrote to Wordsworth on 4 May 1812, '& desired her to judge whether it was possible that a man, who had written such a poem, could be capable of such an act' (*CL* iii. 400). It was nevertheless a remarkably STC-ish thing to do, considering that this was his only fair copy, all the more precious for being in Sara Hutchinson's hand. And sure enough, when he asked for the return of the manuscript on 3 April 1815 (*CL* iv. 564), Lady Beaumont did not send it back. Instead Coleridge received a letter from Wordsworth saying:

Let me beg you out of kindness to me that you would relinquish the intention of publishing the Poem addressed to me after hearing *mine* to you. The commendation would be injurious to us both, and my work, when it appears, would labour under a great disadvantage in consequence of such a precursorship of praise.[3]

Coleridge replied that he had requested the manuscript 'because I was making a *Mss* Collection of *all* my poems, publishable or unpublishable—& still more perhaps for the Handwriting of the only perfect Copy, that entrusted to her Ladyship'.[4] The second point was certainly true, but the first seems disingenuous as, while protesting that he did not intend to publish the poem because of 'it's *personality* respecting myself', Coleridge, having 'lit on the first rude draft, and corrected it as

in *JDC* 525–7 and by William Knight in *Memorials of Coleorton* (Boston, 1897), 213–18. My discussion and citations are based on an examination of the the original mss, and I thank the Dove Cottage Library and the Pierpont Morgan Library for their permission to make use of these. I am also grateful to Professor J. C. C. Mays for his generosity in sharing with me his great knowledge of Coleridge texts in general and of this one in particular.

  [3] Letter, 22 May 1815. Ernest de Selincourt (ed.), *The Letters of William and Dorothy Wordsworth* (2nd edn.), rev. by Mary Moorman and Alan G. Hill, iii. *The Middle Years*, 2 (Oxford: Oxford University Press, 1969), 238.

  [4] Letter, 30 May 1815. *CL* iv. 572. This letter contains Coleridge's transcription of lines 12–47 of the poem.

well as I could', indeed did proceed to publish it, though with its intimate passages revised into less personal ones. J. C. C. Mays has discovered that these changes were made at a very late stage,—in Coleridge's corrections of the *Sibylline Leaves* proofs, and that the readings of the proofs as originally printed were very similar to those of the Sara Hutchinson transcript.[5] Whether Coleridge made these changes out of deference to Wordsworth's feelings or whether they directly reflect his own must remain a matter for speculation.

When the poem appeared in *Sibylline Leaves* in 1817, it attracted little critical notice; but at least one anonymous notice, that in the *Monthly Review* for January 1819, illustrates what Wordsworth had feared: 'The lines to a *Gentleman*, who had recited a poem about the "*growth of an individual mind*", we conclude are verses addressed to Mr. Wordsworth on some nonsensical piece of mysticism, spouted by that flimsy author.'[6] While abuse like this cannot justify the withholding of Coleridge's manuscript, it does show that the apprehensions that Wordsworth had expressed were not groundless. My concern, however, is with the poem itself.

From the beginning of 'To William Wordsworth' Coleridge assumes a self-abnegatory position. His characterization of *The Prelude* as 'That Lay, | More than historic, that prophetic Lay' (2–3), resonates with Coleridge's own failed ambitions. Coleridge too had attempted the 'prophetic Lay' in poems of the 1790s like 'Religious Musings'[7] and the contribution to Robert Southey's *Joan of Arc* later published as 'The Destiny of Nations',[8] poems in which he had indeed been 'Singing of Glory, and Futurity' (78). Indeed, he had gone so far as to say, 'I pin all my credit on Religious Musings.'[9] As Paul Korshin finely remarks, 'Glory and futurity are the stock in trade of the millenarian seer, and the kerygmatic style is the prophet's traditional voice—heraldic and annunicatory'; and in turning his back on these Coleridge relinquishes his former role to Wordsworth.[10] The 'orphic' nature of *The Prelude* is also a quality Coleridge no longer feels capable of attaining. As James Dykes Campbell points out, Coleridge uses this word of Wordsworth's blank

[5] From the apparatus to Mays's forthcoming *CC* edn.

[6] 88 (1819), 24–38. From Donald H. Reiman (ed.), *The Romantics Reviewed*, A. ii. (New York: 1972), 752.

[7] See my ' "These Promised Years": Coleridge's "Religious Musings" and the Millenarianism of the 1790s', in *Revolution and English Romanticism*, ed. Keith Hanley and Raman Selden (Hemel Hempstead: Harvester Wheatsheaf, 1990), 49–66.

[8] See my 'Coleridge's "Preternatural Agency," ' *European Romantic Review*, 1 (1991), 135–46.   [9] Letter to Thomas Poole, 11 Apr. 1796. *CL* i. 203.

[10] Korshin, *Typologies in England: 1660–1820* (Princeton, NJ: Princeton University Press, 1982) 388–9.

verse elsewhere. In his 'Notes on Barclay's Argenis'[11] Coleridge distinguishes the orphic from the epic, the dramatic, the lyric, and the colloquial. 'Of what may be called Orphic, or philosophic, blank verse,' he says, 'perfect models may be found in Wordsworth'[12] In 'To William Wordsworth' he wrote:

> —An Orphic Song indeed,
> A song divine of high and passionate thoughts
> To their own music chaunted!
>
> (45–7)

Coleridge used these lines, with only a slight variation, to introduce a passage from *The Prelude* in *The Friend*,[13] but when he applied it to his own work it was with a significant difference. The lines occur in Chapter 13 of the *Biographia Literaria*, in the letter that Coleridge wrote to himself describing what his projected work on the Imagination would be like:

> —An orphic tale, indeed,
> A tale *obscure* of high and passionate thoughts
> To a *strange* music chaunted!
>
> (i. 302)

By italicizing the variants, Coleridge emphasizes the difference between divine and obscure, and between the eccentricity of his 'chaunting' of thoughts to a 'strange music' and the centrality of Wordsworth's chanting them to their own. The Bardic nature that Coleridge assigns to Wordsworth in lines 48 and 83 constitutes one more implied contrast: in the early 'Songs of the Pixies' Coleridge had called himself a Bard (36), but now that title too has been transferred to Wordsworth.

In celebrating Wordsworth's accomplishment and denigrating his own, Coleridge employs several discursive strategies. One is what Lucy Newlyn has aptly called, in discussing the work of both poets, a language of allusion.[14] This sometimes involves associations with *The Prelude*, sometimes with his own past works. For example, in referring to 'vital breathings' (9) Coleridge, using a word that appears in only one other poem of his own,[15] was aware that words associated with breath are a

---

[11] *Poetical Works*, 634.

[12] Henry Nelson Coleridge (ed.), *The Literary Remains of Samuel Taylor Coleridge*, i (London, 1836), 256.

[13] no. 19, 28 Dec. 1809. *Friend* ii. 259. Republished 1818 (*Friend* i. 368). The only variant is 'Tale' for 'Song', and that is the reading of both manuscripts.

[14] Newlyn, *Coleridge, Wordsworth, and the Language of Allusion* (Oxford: The Clarendon Press, 1986).

[15] See Sr. Eugenia Logan, *A Concordance to the Poetry of Coleridge* (Saint Mary-of-the Woods, Ind., privately printed, 1940), 82. The other occurrence is in 'Frost at Midnight'.

staple of Wordsworth's poetic vocabulary, as in 'Breathings for incom-
municable powers' (*Prelude* iii. 188). Coleridge emphasized that such
words in *The Prelude* suggest the oracular when, writing to Wordsworth
about the poem, he quoted Aristophanes: 'Indeed thro' the whole of
that poem "*Breathed o'er me too: a very mystic whiff*." '[16] 'Breathings' is,
then, an appropriation of a Wordsworthian term for purposes both poets
understood. Alternatively, Coleridge draws upon a discourse he shared
with Wordsworth, as in 'some inner Power' (16) and 'when power
streamed from thee' (18), references that come trailing clouds of rich
associations for both. As the poem continues, Coleridge reconstitutes
episodes from *The Prelude* for an original audience almost as conversant
with the poem as its author. He even replicates some of the characteristic cadences of *The Prelude*, as Thomas McFarland has pointed out;[17]
and he introduces material peculiar to his own earlier poetry, once more
with the expectations of audience recognition. Later on, these elements
are reinforced by allusions to Milton's 'Lycidas' and to the Gospels.
What all these methods have in common is the motive of establishing
radical differences between himself and Wordsworth and between his
own past and present identities, culminating in the poet's ritual death as
a sacrifice to his subject. In drawing out the themes of *The Prelude,* as
both Tilottama Rajan and Lucy Newlyn have observed, Coleridge is
highly selective, giving special prominence to Wordsworth's periods in
France and his experience of the French Revolution.[18] 'For thou wert
there, thine own brows garlanded' (33), for instance, refers to the cele-
brations at which Wordsworth was a guest after arriving in France on
the first anniversary of the fall of the Bastille; but in *The Prelude* vi.
355–413 Wordsworth emphasizes the distance he then felt from the
Revolutionary celebrants, and it is Coleridge who has supplied the garland, in order to imply a contrast with himself. After the early 'Songs of
the Pixies' (in which the poet himself wears 'the future garland'),
Coleridge tends to represent himself as making wreaths for others, as in
'To Matilda Betham from a Stranger' (29–30).

> A coronal, which, with undoubting hand,
> I twine around the brows of patriot HOPE!
> (*CPW* i. 375)

[16] 30 May 1815. *CL* iv. 572.

[17] McFarland, *Romanticism and the Forms of Ruin: Wordsworth, Coleridge, and the Modalities of Fragmentation* (Princeton, NJ: Princeton University Press, 1981), 59–60. 'Hardly anywhere else,' McFarland comments, 'does Coleridge achieve this peculiar Miltonicity of style in which *The Prelude's* great moments are couched.'

[18] Rajan, *The Supplement of Reading* (Ithaca, NY: Cornell University Press, 1980), 126. Newlyn, *Coleridge, Wordsworth, and the Language of Allusion*, 196.

Much later, he would picture his own brow as 'wreathless' in 'Work without Hope'. Furthermore, the Dove Cottage manuscript emphasizes the communal nature of the observance:

> Mid festive Crowds, *thy* brows too garlanded,
> A Brother of the Feast . . .
>
> (DCL, 16–17)

One may think of an antithetical figure lingering outside a bridal feast, a link which becomes virtually explicit in lines 29–30, where 'France in all her town lay vibrating | Like some becalmed bark'. 'The ship hath been suddenly becalmed', says the marginal gloss to *The Rime of the Ancient Mariner* (*CPW* i. 190); and, of course, even without the gloss the deadly calm takes up much of the central part of that poem. Further echoes of Coleridge's most famous creation will occur later in 'To William Wordsworth'.

As we have seen, Coleridge establishes both parallel and contrastive meanings by drawing upon elements of Wordsworthian diction or, alternatively, upon a shared vocabulary. A new discursive strategy is introduced in lines 36–43, where Coleridge reverts to the trope that had dominated his early poetry: personification. Personification had been politely shown the door in the 1800 Preface to *Lyrical Ballads*:

Except in a very few instances the Reader will find no personification of abstract ideas in these volumes, not that I mean to censure such personifications: they may well be fitted for certain kinds of composition, but in these poems I propose to imitate, and as far as possible to adopt the very language of men, and I do not find that such personifications make any regular or natural part of that language.[19]

For a short time, Coleridge's most important poems were largely free of personifications, but it became part of his strategy of recuperation to re-introduce the figures most that once been most congenial to his early sensibility. A way of reclaiming poetic territory that had been his before his association with Wordsworth, Coleridge's practice here is intimately linked with the theme of recovering or at least compensating for aspects of a lost artistic identity. This had begun as early as 1798 with 'France: An Ode', in which personification is the chief mode of figuration. In 'To William Wordsworth' we find a personification so extended as to become an almost mythical presence in lines 36–44, beginning:

> When from the general heart of human kind
> Hope sprang forth like a full-born Deity!

---

[19] Wordsworth and Coleridge, *Lyrical Ballads 1798*, ed. W. J. B. Owen (2nd edn., London: Oxford University Press, 1980), 160–1.

The power of this image is intensified in the Morgan Library manuscript, where 'Hope sprang forth, an armed Deity!' creates an even closer link with some of Coleridge's earlier poems.

The personification of the French Revolution as a powerful female being is a conspicuous feature in Coleridge's earlier work.[20] In the sonnet 'To Earl Stanhope', published in the *Poems* of 1796, she 'from the Almighty's bosom leapt | With whirlwind arm, fierce minister of Love!' (*CPW* i. 90). To leave no doubt, Coleridge footnoted the character as 'Gallic Liberty'. A similarly Amazonian figure appears in 'To A Young Lady with a Poem on the French Revolution', written in 1794:

> Fierce on her front the blasting Dog-star glow'd;
> Her banners, like a midnight meteor, flow'd;
> Amid the yelling of the storm-rent skies!
> She came, and scatter'd battles from her eyes!
>
> (*CPW* i. 65, ll. 19–22)

In 'Preternatural Agency', Coleridge's contribution to Southey's *Joan of Arc*, she is 'A dazzling form, broad-bosomed, bold of eye, | And wild her hair, save where with laurels bound'.[21] Even in the palinode 'France' she is still redoubtable, 'When insupportably advancing, | Her arm made mockery of the warrior's ramp' (53–4). In 'To William Wordsworth' this figure of revolutionary Hope militant is transformed:

> —Of that dear Hope afflicted and struck down,
> So summon'd homeward, thenceforth calm and sure
> From the dread watch-tower of man's absolute self,
> With light unwaning on her eyes, to look
> Far on—herself a glory to behold,
> The Angel of the vision!

Even some of this poem's most astute readers[22] have taken 'summon'd homeward' to apply to Wordsworth, but the passage would then be ungrammatical, since one cannot be 'afflicted and struck down of that dear Hope'. The passage is actually anaphoric, parallel to the 'Of' phrases that begin lines 12, 20, and 27, all four being governed by 'Theme hard as high!' in line 11. (The meaning would have been more

---

[20] See my 'Apocalypse and Millennium in the Poetry of Coleridge', *The Wordsworth Circle*, 23 (1992), 24–34.

[21] ll. 433–4 of *The Destiny of Nations* version; *CPW* i. 146.

[22] Among those reading the homeward journey as Wordsworth's are Parker, in *Coleridge's Meditative Art* (Ithaca, NY: Cornell University Press, 1975), 230, and Rajan (*The Supplement of Reading*, 136). M. H. Abrams interprets the lines as applying to Hope, *Natural Supernaturalism: Tradition and Revolution in Romantic Literature* (New York: W. W. Norton, 1971), 458.

immediately evident in the plural 'Themes' that was originally the reading of the PML MS). One aspect of Wordsworth's 'theme' is that Hope, afflicted and struck down by the failure of the French Revolution, has been transferred to the interior life of the prophetic poet. The Dove Cottage manuscript makes this even more explicit, with 'Thence summon'd homeward—homeward to thy Heart' (DCL 33), instead of the 'thenceforth calm and sure' of the other versions. In that manuscript, though the birth of Hope is absent, there is also a more extensive treatment of her tribulations preceding the 'homeward' journey:

> Ah! soon night roll'd on night, and every Cloud
> Open'd its' eye of Fire: and Hope aloft
> Now flutter'd, and now toss'd upon the Storm
> Floating!
>
> (DCL 28–31)

The manuscript then connects with line 38 of the published version. From then on, Hope looks 'far on' from 'the dread watch-tower of man's absolute self'; yet what is most important is not what she sees but her own transformation: 'herself a glory to behold, | The angel of the vision!' As critics have remarked, there is an echo here of 'the great vision of the guarded mount' in *Lycidas* 161[23]. At the same time it has a peculiarly Coleridgean meaning.

In *Dejection: An Ode* the poet tells the Lady:

> Ah! from the soul itself must issue forth
> A light, a glory, a fair luminous cloud—;
> Enveloping the Earth—
>
> (ll. 53–5).

In both contexts 'glory' suggests the aureole or nimbus radiating from a figure in sacred art. Hope in 'To William Wordsworth', 'with light unwaning on her eyes', achieves the same self-referentiality as the *schöne Seele* of 'Dejection'. Much later, Coleridge returned to the 'Angel of the Vision' in a Notebook passage probably written in 1826 (NB 26, BL Add MS 47524):

Is there a man who has [strongly sensed *del.*] truly and intensely loved a lovely and beautiful Woman, a Woman capable of gazing, in that inward [most *del.*] communion of Silence, on Vale, Lake, and Mountain Forest, in the richness of

---

[23] See e.g. Parker, *Coleridge's Meditative Art*, 230; editorial note to the Norton Critical Edition of *The Prelude 1799, 1805, 1850*, ed. Jonathan Wordsworth, M. H. Abrams, and Stephen Gill (New York: Norton, 1979), 543; and Jean-Pierre Mileur, *Vision and Revision: Coleridge's Art of Immanence* (Berkeley: University of California Press, 1982), 125–6.

a rising or a setting Sun, [herself *del.*] she as she stands by his side smitten by the radiance, 'herself a glory to behold, the Angel of the Vision.'[24]

This Notebook passage brings together object of desire and personified abstraction in one self-allusive quotation. Yet when Coleridge imagines himself or a surrogate self in such a context it is with a real—that is to say, fantasied—woman troped into the Angel. In his figuration of Wordsworth, however, the feminine personification becomes internalized by the prophetic poet alone.

The next verse paragraph, the fourth in the published versions, begins with an elevated tribute to Wordsworth's accomplishment, followed by a contrastive, mythologized view of Coleridge's failure. These are linked in the DCL and PML manuscripts, but not in any version published during Coleridge's lifetime, by an intimate passage of fifteen lines:

> Dear shall it be to every human Heart,
> To me how more than dearest! Me, on whom
> Comfort from thee, and utterance of thy Love,
> Came with such heights and depths of harmony,
> Such sense of Wings uplifting, that the Storm
> Scatter'd and whirl'd me, till my Thoughts became
> A bodily Tumult! and thy faithful Hopes,
> Thy Hopes of me, dear Friend! by me unfelt
> Were troublous to me, almost as a Voice,
> Familiar once and more than Musical;
> To one cast forth, whose hope had seem'd to die,
> A Wanderer with a worn-out heart,
> Mid Strangers pining with untended Wounds!
>
> O Friend! too well thou know'st, of what sad years
> The long suppression had benumm'd my soul . . .[25]

Coleridge's consciousness of 'Thy Hope of me, dear Friend!' puts him in the situation of the struggling Hope of the preceding section; now

[24] I am grateful to Tim Fulford for drawing my attention to this passage and to Mary Anne Perkins for helping me locate it. 'The angel of the vision' also appears in Don Alvar's description of Teresa in *Remorse* I. i. 54. Coleridge noted in the copy he gave Sara Hutchinson: 'May not a man, without breach of the 8th commandment, take out of his left pocket and put into his right?' See *CPW* ii. 821 and n.

[25] DCL ms, ll. 54–69. PML transcript, 62–76. The PML transcript has a number of variants, including one important revision in Coleridge's (not Sara Hutchinson's) hand, where the 11th line, originally as in the DCL ms., has been deleted and 'As a dear Woman's voice to one cast forth' substituted. This change must have been made later than 23 Nov. 1809, as a note by B. Graves accompanying the PML transcript argues (on the basis of a passage from *The Friend*, discussed below). Coleridge must of course have imagined the 'dear voice' as Sara's.

it is he who is 'whirl'd' by the storm. The hopes expressed in the lines Wordsworth read were 'troublous' in the same way that Coleridge's reading of Book 6 in MS B led him to make corrections, he noted, 'for the purpose of the deadening of a too strong feeling, which the personal Passages, so exquisitely beautiful, had excited'.[26] Now Coleridge projects himself in images of the victim and/or outcast, conflating aspects of William Cowper's Castaway—'One cast forth, whose hope had seem'd to die'; his own Ancient Mariner—'A Wanderer with a worn-out heart', and the man who had fallen among thieves in Luke 10: 30, 'Mid Strangers pining with untended Wounds!' As the manuscript passage merges back into the printed text at line 63 with 'Even as Life returns upon the drowned', this composite figure gains another dimension.

Line 63 is, as George Whalley has pointed out, yet another echo of *The Rime of the Ancient Mariner*: 'Like one that hath been seven days drowned | My body lay afloat'.[27] At the same time, as is widely recognized, this is a reference to the drowned Lycidas, who now becomes yet another of Coleridge's mythical manifestations—drowned, his body displayed on a flower-strewn bier, and resurrected.[28] In lines 65–75, lines that Coleridge would later reproduce with an ambiguous mixture of self-exculpation and self-accusation in the *Biographia Literaria* (i. 221–2), there is a grotesque irony that fails to mask the poet's aggression towards his subject: the flowers on the coffin are those that were culled by Coleridge himself or that, reared by his patient toil, 'had opened out' in his 'Commune' with Wordsworth. '—That way no more!' in line 82 seems a desperate attempt to prevent the poem from voicing the accusation, 'I am dead and it's you who have killed me'. Even so, when Coleridge asks Wordsworth not to 'impair the memory of that hour | Of thy communion with my nobler mind' (83–4), it does seem, especially if we note the use of the word 'injure' rather than 'impair' in DCL line 89, as if Coleridge fears Wordsworth will do just that. In order to deflect such implications, Coleridge introduces another layer of intertextuality in the latter part of the poem.

What we have, up to this point, is Coleridge's awareness that, as Stephen Gill puts it, 'his poem lays bare the latent tensions and

---

[26] See *The Prelude or Growth of a Poet's Mind*, ed. Ernest de Selincourt, 2nd edn. rev. Helen Darbishire (Oxford: The Clarendon Press, 1959), 559.

[27] *CPW* i. 207, ll. 553–5. See *Coleridge and Sara Hutchinson* (Toronto: University of Toronto Press, 1955), 117.

[28] See Parker, *Coleridge's Meditative Art*, 233–8; Mileur, *Vision and Revision*, 128–9; Newlyn, *Coleridge, Wordsworth, and the Language of Allusion*, 199.

ambivalences of the situation'.[29] This is not the place to go into the psychodynamics of the Wordsworth–Coleridge relationship, a subject already fruitfully explored. As Thomas McFarland argues, in Wordsworth and Coleridge's 'symbiosis', Coleridge played the sublimated role of the masochistic partner.[30] There were undoubtedly matters such as the removal of *Christabel* from *Lyrical Ballads* that at least subconsciously complicated Coleridge's reverence for Wordsworth, but it is not the *sub*conscious that concerns us here. At the time of writing 'To William Wordsworth', Coleridge was consciously, vehemently, and one must say pathologically jealous of his friend, as the evidence of his Notebooks witnesses. Coleridge was convinced that Wordsworth and Sara Hutchinson had been in bed together at the Queen's Head, near Coleorton, on 27 December 1806 at precisely 10. 50 a.m. (*CN* ii. 2975 and n.). Much later, he recognized his belief as a 'mere phantasm', but there can be no question that he was suffering from what he later called 'the lancinations of positive Jealousy' (*CN* 2: 2975 n.) during the very period in which he wrote 'To William Wordsworth'. His feeling of being supplanted as a poet by Wordsworth is intertwined with his fantasy of being supplanted as a man. In order to turn the poem into the celebration it had announced itself as being, its subject must by analogy be translated to another realm, while the poet himself undergoes a at least a partial resurrection.

A little earlier, in lines 49–54, Coleridge had made the first of a series of New Testament analogies involving Wordsworth:

> With stedfast eye I viewed thee in the choir
> Of ever-enduring men. The truly great
> Have all one age, and from one visible space
> Shed influence! They, both in power and act,
> Are permanent, and Time is not with them,
> Save as it worketh for them, they in it.

In so locating Wordsworth in a timeless realm, Coleridge places him in an only partially secularized version of the community of saints, the 'just men made perfect' of Heb. 12: 22–3:

But ye are come unto Mount Sion and unto the city of the living God, the heavenly Jerusalem, And to an innumerable company of angels.

To the general assembly and church of the firstborn, which are written in heaven, and to God the Judge of all, and to the spirits of just men made perfect.

[29] Gill, *William Wordsworth: A Life* (Oxford: Clarendon Press, 1989), 255. *Cf.* Lucy Newlyn's statement that 'there can be no doubt that his admiration for *The Prelude* is qualified by bitterness' (*Coleridge, Wordsworth, and the Language of Allusion*, 195).

[30] McFarland, *Romanticism and the Forms of Ruin*, 69.

This begins an intertexture of New Testament references taken up again in lines 77–8, where Coleridge characterizes himself as one 'Who came a welcomer in herald's guise, | Singing of Glory and Futurity'. Wordsworth had used sacred analogies in a similar way in describing, in *The Prelude*, his transfer of loyalty from nation to Revolution:

> . . . patriotic love
> Did of itself in modesty give way
> Like the precursor when the deity
> Is come, whose harbinger he is . . .
>   (x. 280–3)

Behind both statements is the figure of John the Baptist, who described himself as preparing the way for Jesus, and who declared in Luke 3: 16, 'One mightier than I cometh.' (Significantly, Wordsworth would reject such 'a precursorship of praise' when asking Coleridge not to publish 'To William Wordsworth'.) The poem goes on to hail Wordsworth as the Christ of Palm Sunday, with 'triumphal wreaths | Strew'd before thy advancing!' (81–2), as in Matt. 21: 8, 'Others cut down branches from the trees, and strawed them in the way.' Then, while expressing a profound personal feeling in addressing Wordsworth as 'my comforter!' in line 102, Coleridge dramatically changes their mutual roles to those of Jesus and the Holy Ghost in John 16: 7: 'It is expedient for you that I go away: for if I do not go away, the Comforter will not come unto you; but if I depart, I will send him unto you.' Coleridge's death becomes analogous to that of Jesus, creating a space in which the Holy Spirit in the form of Wordsworth may live among men.

Death is followed by resurrection, though for Coleridge it is a partial one. This process begins with 'Even as Life returns upon the drowned' in line 63, as a result of hearing Wordsworth's reading of *The Prelude*. It continues with Coleridge's finding himself in a state propitious for the reception, and by implication, for the creation of poetry.

> In silence listening, like a devout child,
> My soul lay passive, by the various strain
> Driven as in surges now beneath the stars,
> With momentary stars of my own birth,
> Fair constelled foam, still darting off
> Into the darknes; now a tranquil sea,
> Outspread and bright, yet swelling to the moon.
>   (ll. 95–100)

Coleridge's association of the moon with the poetic imagination has been so much discussed that it needs no further comment here. The

passage also has a parallel in the beginning of the homeward journey in
Part VI of *The Rime of the Ancient Mariner*:

> Still as a slave before his lord,
> The ocean has no blast;
> His great bright eye most silently
> Up to the Moon is cast—
>
> (ll. 414–17)

Another parallel is that noted by Coleridge himself. In *Sibylline Leaves*
he added a note, which he had also inserted at the end of the PML MS,
to 'constellated', citing *The Friend*:

A beautiful white cloud of Foam at momentary intervals coursed by the side of
the Vessel with a Roar, and little stars of flame danced and sparkled and went
out in it: and every now and then light detachments of of this white cloud-like
foam darted off from the vessel's side, each with its own small constellation,
over the Sea, and scoured out of sight like a Tartar Troop over a Wilderness.[31]

On this passage Geoffrey Hill, who compares the gloss about 'the jour-
neying Moon', and 'the stars that still sojourn, yet still move onward' in
Part IV of *The Rime of the Ancient Mariner*, perceptively comments:

Flux is redrawn as harmonious motion towards rest; and rest is seen as active
contemplation, not as stagnation. The mariner knows enough of stagnation;
the stars are of another order. And in the poem 'To William Wordsworth', the
private utterance of highly organized art can for a while stabilize the self-
dissipating brilliance of the listener's mind, that is, Coleridge's mind, the mind
that is concentrating upon that very diffusion. It is a transfiguring of weakness
into strength.[32]

The passage works on several levels. It links Coleridge once more to his
greatest poem, a poem in which fall is followed by redemption; and it
creates yet another parallel between its central figure and himself. And
it also recapitulates the process of its own creation, introducing, in so
doing, the element of creativity. Neither the passage in *The Friend* nor
the letter to Mrs Sara Coleridge on which it is based (3 October 1798;
CL i. 1204–5) employ the expression 'stars of my own birth'. That is
found only in this poem, a reminder of the creative fecundity with
which Coleridge shaped the foam into stars, and a promise—or at least
a hint—that this power still remains with him.

---

[31] *Sibylline Leaves*, repr. (Oxford: Woodstock Books, 1990) 202 n.; *The Friend*, 14 (23 Nov.
1809), ii. 220.
[32] *The Lords of Limit: Essays on Literature and Ideas* (New York: Oxford University Press,
1984), 12. I thank Tim Fulford for bringing this essay to my attention.

'To William Wordsworth' concludes with one last analogy of Coleridge to his Ancient Mariner: 'And when I rose, I found myself in prayer.' The Mariner blessed the water-snakes 'unaware' and found that 'The self-same moment I could pray' (ll. 285, 288), a necessary prelude to the return that would enable the telling of his tale. Coleridge's response to Wordsworth's reading enables him to write the poem that, as Newton Stallknecht suggests, brings him back to life from spiritual death,[33] thus leaving him room for the telling of his own tale. That tale, that future poetry, was no longer to be in the vatic mode that distinguished his greatest earlier poems. The prophetic poet lies self-interred, but the concluding part of 'To William Wordsworth' adumbrates a different role for its author as a poet of personal sentiment, intimate friendship, and meditative reflection. This poetry to come would not make the claims of 'major' poetry, and it would be rendered in a more discursive style. Prosopopeia, so dramatically revived with the figure of Hope, would be its dominant trope. It would make contact with Coleridge's early poetry both in figuration and in subject matter, yet it would be distinctively 'later'. At about the time of composing 'To William Wordsworth', Coleridge made a modest beginning in this direction by reworking an early poem which Sara Hutchinson then inscribed in her album,[34] a poem that indicates the direction of Coleridge's later poetry.

'Hope and Time' / 'Time, Real and Imaginary'

Hope, whose allegorized history plays such an important role in 'To William Wordsworth', is also a theme of the poem known by the editorial title of 'Hope and Time' (*Poems*, 388).[35] A somewhat different version of the second part of this 26-line manuscript poem later appeared in *Sibylline Leaves* as the 11-line 'Time, Real and Imaginary/An Allegory' (*CPW* i. 419–20). Coleridge did not include this poem in the body of *Sibylline Leaves* but rather among three preliminary poems (pp. v–vi) that precede the rest, and in the Preface (p. iii) he refers to it as one of 'two school-boy poems' (the other being 'The Raven'). This dating has long been the cause of controversy. James Dykes Campbell

---

[33] Stallknecht, *Strange Seas of Thought* (2nd edn., Bloomington, Ind.: University of Indiana Press, 1962), p. xi. For other views of the poem's conclusion see Newlyn, *Coleridge, Wordsworth, and the Language of Allusion*, 202; Mileur, *Vision and Revision*, 128.

[34] This album is generally known as 'Sara Hutchinson's Poets'. For dating see Whalley, *Coleridge and Sara Hutchinson*, 130–1.   [35] Ibid., 130–2, Beer, *Poems*, 388.

maintained long ago, 'These lines may embody some school-boy dream of holidays and his sister Anne; it may even have received some shape in boyhood—but not its present shape—that must have been impressed at a later date' (*JDC* 638). Whalley argues convincingly that that later date coincides with the Coleorton visit, but distinguishes between the 'text' and the 'allegory' in making the point that 'whatever the history of the text, the allegory has a Christ's Hospital origin'.[36] It is clear that the poem marked an epoch for Coleridge in some special sense. We may argue from internal evidence what that particular importance was, but it is interesting to find corroboration from an external source. The astronomer William Rowan Hamilton visited Coleridge at Highgate in 1832, and later told his biographer:

While Coleridge spoke in a very depreciatory tone of that elegy of his on an infant, he also spoke with comparative, and indeed (I think) with positive satisfaction, of another very youthful poem of his own, entitled, 'Time, Real and Imaginary', which is also among his published works. He repeated this poem with some enthusiasm, and spoke of it as proving a truly remarkable advance of his own mind (and perhaps of his poetical powers) towards maturity, in the year (or some such period) which had elapsed between the dates of the two compositions.[37]

We can now understand Coleridge's motives for recasting his early poem at Coleorton, for adding an introductory section longer than the the revised poem, for inscribing a version of the whole in Sara Hutchinson's album, and for printing 'Time, Real and Imaginary' as 'a schoolboy poem' in *Sibylline Leaves*. For him the original poem represented his breakthrough from a general period style to an early style recognizably his own. He now prepares to write new poems, moving from the basis of that earlier style, bridging past and present. Yet his attitude toward his own poetic rebirth is complex, for he recognizes that readers are likely to contrast productions like this one to his greatest works. The fourteen lines prefixed to the allegory are therefore apologetic to the point of undermining it.

[36] *Coleridge and Sara Hutchinson*, 131. Campbell suggested the date as *c*.1815 while *Sibylline Leaves* was being prepared, and EHC dated it ?1812, but whether the version in *Sara Hutchinson's Poets* (ll. 15–25) is earlier or later than the poem in *Sibylline Leaves*, the transcription cannot have been made after the rift with Wordsworth in 1810.

[37] Robert Perceval Graves, *Life of Sir William Rowan Hamilton*, i (London and Dublin, 1882), 541. The other poem, 'Epitaph on an Infant', has generally been dated 1794 (*CPW* i. 68, *Poems*, 39) because of its appearance in the *Morning Chronicle* in that year, but if the reference to it here as 'a short and juvenile poem' (i. 540) has any meaning, it must have been written earlier.

Coleridge begins with a myth of origins intended to account for whatever deficiencies the allegory may have by the deficiencies of his own urban boyhood:

> In the great City rear'd, my fancy rude
> By natural Forms unnurs'd & unsubdued,
> An Alien from the Rivers & the Fields
> And all the Charms, that Hill or Woodland yields . . .

As Whalley notes, this is the view of the boy Coleridge to be found in *The Prelude* and in Charles Lamb's 'Christ's Hospital Five-and-Thirty Years Ago'. It is a view that Coleridge himself had previously expressed:

> For I was reared
> In the great city, pent 'mid cloisters dim,
> And saw nought lovely but the sky and stars.
> ('Frost At Midnight', 51–3)

> At eve, star-gazing in 'ecstatic fit'
> (Alas! for cloister'd in a city School
> The Sky was all, I knew, of Beautiful)
> At the barr'd window often did I sit,
> And oft upon the leaded School-roof lay . . .
> ('Letter to Sara Hutchinson', 62–6)

In Book vi of *The Prelude*, which, as we have seen, meant so much to Coleridge, Wordsworth draws on this myth of urban imprisonment:

> Of Rivers, Fields,
> And Groves, I speak to thee, my Friend; to thee,
> Who, yet a liveried School-Boy, in the depths
> Of the huge City, on the leaded Roof
> Of that wide Edifice, thy home and School,
> Wast used to lie and gaze upon the clouds
> Moving in Heaven; or haply, tired of this,
> To shut thine eyes, and by internal light
> See trees, and meadows, and thy native Stream
> Far distant, thus beheld from year to year
> Of thy long exile.[38]

Coleridge says he was 'rear'd' in the great city because his origin was elsewhere. As Charles Lamb would put it in his fictionalized re-creation:

---

[38] ll. 274–84. In his *Oxford Authors* edn. of Wordsworth, Stephen Gill suggests that 'thy native Stream' refers not only to the actual River Otter but also to Coleridge's early 'Sonnet | To the River Otter'. *William Wordsworth* (Oxford: Oxford University Press, 1990 [1984]), 732.

O the cruelty of separating a poor lad from his early homestead! The yearnings which I used to have towards it in those unfledged years! How, in my dreams, would my native town (far in the west) come back, with its church, and trees, and faces! How I would wake weeping, and in the anguish of my heart exclaim upon sweet Calne in Wiltshire![39]

Coleridge's own attitude toward Christ's Hospital was not always so dismissive, as his account in the *Biographia Literaria* testifies, and one senses that he remained proud of his poems inscribed in James Boyer's *Liber Aureus*. However, it suits his purpose here to make the lack of a Ministry of Love and a Ministry of Fear, 'By natural Forms unnurs'd and unsubdued', account for the secondary nature of the poetry he produced then and will produce now.

'Hope and Time' continues with a curiously ambivalent account of the poetry Coleridge wrote at Christ's Hospital.

> It was the pride & passion of my Youth
> T''impersonate and color moral Truth [:]
> Rare Allegories in those Days I spun,
> That oft had mystic senses oft'ner none.

'Impersonate' here has the primary meaning of 'personify', yet a certain residue of false identity remains; and 'color' also suggests falsification, especially when it is 'moral truth' that is to be coloured. Yet a poet must necessarily employ tropes and 'colors' of rhetoric. What Coleridge is doing here is disarming potential criticism by lowering the reader's expectations, a strategy that has been discussed in the Introduction to this book. His 'Rare Allegories' are equivocal in value even before we reach the following, undermining line; allegory was to Coleridge a secondary mode *per se*, as he was to state explicitly in a celebrated passage of *The Statesman's Manual*:

The mechanical understanding . . . in the blindness of self-complacency confounds SYMBOLS with ALLEGORIES. Now an Allegory is but a translation of abstract notions into a picture-language, which is itself nothing but an abstraction from objects of the senses; the principal being more worthless even than its phantom proxy, both alike unsubstantial. On the other hand a symbol . . . is characterized by a translucence of the Special in the Individual or of the General in the Especial or of the Universal in the General. Above all by the translucence of the Special of the Eternal through and in the Temporal. It always partakes of the Reality which it renders intelligible; and while it enunciates the

---

[39] 'Christ's Hospital Five-and Thirty Years Ago' (1820). Augustine Birrell (ed.), *The Essays of Elia* (London: J. M. Dent, 1907), 15. Coleridge of course was born in Ottery St Mary, Devon., but the intended parallel is clear.

whole, abides itself as a living part in that Unity, of which it is the representative. The other are but empty echoes which the fancy arbitrarily associates with apparitions of matter.[40]

This was published, of course, in 1816, but the denigration of allegory is consistent with earlier statements. In 1795, for example, Coleridge said of the Gnostics: 'The Philosopher invading the province of the Poet endeavoured to strike and dazzle by bold Fiction, and allegoric personification.[41] The poems of Coleridge's great period were characterized by symbolism; those following could at best provide a phantom proxy. Yet, whatever Coleridge's theoretical attitude might be, in practice he made allegory a signature of his later poetry. In the *Sibylline Leaves* version of *The Rime of the Ancient Mariner*, the figures in the spectre-bark are for the first time allegorized. 'That woman and her fleshless Pheere,' actors in a Gothic drama in the 1798 version, become 'the Nightmare LIFE-IN-DEATH' and 'DEATH' (*CPW* i. 193–4). Later still, 'The Pang More Sharp Than All' would be subtitled 'An Allegory' and 'Love's Apparition and Evanishment' 'An Allegorical Romance' (see Ch. 4). By the time he wrote 'Hope and Time', Coleridge had returned to 'Rare Allegories', however unwilling he may have been to justify them.

As 'Hope and Time' continues, the poet's statements about his production become so dismissive that the reader is led to wonder why he wrote the poem at all when it is merely 'Of commonest Thoughts a moving Masquerade', an exercise in mystification, both 'obscure and uncouth'. In *Sibylline Leaves* Coleridge is able to deflect responsibility to 'the request of the friends of my youth' (*CPW* i. 419 n.). Whether or not such requests were made, this is an enabling fiction that permits him to print the poem without further justification. In 'Hope and Time' a similar purpose is served by the characterization of the text that follows as 'A sort of Emblem', introducing a puzzle element that we know appealed to the poet and that could be expected to attract the reader as well. Coleridge had a virtually lifelong interest in emblems and emblem literature, to the extent that George Whalley has classified one group of his poems as 'Emblem Poems' because of 'the heraldic isolation and heraldic specificity of their central images'.[42] Unlike the

---

[40] *Lay Sermons*, 30.

[41] *Lectures 1795*, 197. *Cf.* the discussion of allegory, which has its germ in a Notebook entry of 1807–8 (*CN* ii. 3203), in the *Lectures on European Literature* of 1818: although beauty is granted to some allegory, 'it is incapable of exciting any lively interest for any length of time'; Spenser's allegory is boring, while Bunyan's succeeds only because we forget that it is allegory and read it as we would a novel. *Lectures 1808–19*, ii. 102–3.

[42] ' "Late Autumn's Amaranth": Coleridge's Late Poems', 174–5.

symbol, which may refuse to yield its meaning at all, an emblem is known to have a single, denotative meaning. It both mystifies and teases, promising the reader the kind of satisfaction that comes from solving an acrostic. As presented in 'Hope and Time', the text does exhibit such characteristics, but in the *Sibylline Leaves* version matters are a little different, and it may be questioned whether the puzzle is soluble at all.

'In ancient Days, but when I have not read, | Nor know I, where' begins the manuscript version. This places the scene in a distinctly literary realm, about which the author makes the customary disclaimer. The printed versions, however, begin 'On the wide level of a mountain's head', making the site an imagined landscape rather than a text. The use of the word 'faery' instead of 'elfish' in the next line introduces a key word that has a special meaning to Coleridge, who later defined Spenser's 'Land of Faery' as 'mental space',[43] and would use the word significantly in 'The Garden of Boccaccio' and other late poems (see Ch. 3). The children's 'ostrich-like' wings—whether 'pennons' as in the manuscript, or 'pinions' as in *Sibylline Leaves*—employed almost grotesquely as 'sails outspread', will require further comment. Nothing is uncertain about their identities in 'Sara's Poets': the sister is Hope outrunning her brother Time and looking back for him. In *Sibylline Leaves*, however, the figures are unnamed. Which is Time Real and which Time Imaginary, and what is their relation to Hope and Time? At first this may seem almost self-explanatory. Time Imaginary would presumably outrun Time Real, and they would then correspond, respectively, to Hope and Time. Yet why should either Hope or Time Imaginary look backward? Coleridge's own remark in the Preface to *Sibylline Leaves* was evidently meant to clarify this.

By imaginary Time, I meant the state of a school boy's mind when on his return from school he projects his being in his day dreams, and lives in his next holidays, six months hence; and this I contrasted with real Time.

(*CPW* i. 419 n.)

Yet, though we may be disposed to see the inhabitant of real time as blind, not seeing beyond the immediate situation, this hardly explains why imaginary Time looks back, and with such evident anxiety.

Scholars beginning with E. H. Coleridge have looked to Coleridge's Notebooks for a gloss on this poem, most notably to an entry of 1811:

---

[43] 'Lectures on Shakespeare &c.', *Lectures 1808–19* ii. 409–10. See Jeanie Watson, *Risking Enchantment: Coleridge's Symbolic World of Faery* (Lincoln, Nebr: University of Nebraska Press, 1990), 55.

Contrast of troubled manhood, and joyously-active youth, in the sense of Time. To the former [it *del*.] Time, like the Sun in a [cloud *del*.] empty Sky is never seen to move, but only to *have moved*—there, there it was—& now tis here—now distant—yet all a blank between/To the latter it is as the full moon in a fine breezy October night—driving on amid Clouds of all shapes and hues & kindling shifting colors, like an Ostrich in its speed—& yet seems not to have moved at all—This I feel to be a just image of time real & time as felt, in two different states of Being—the Title of the Poem therefore (for Poem it ought to be) should be Time real and Time felt (in the sense of Time) in Active Youth/ or Activity and Hope & fullness of aim in any period/and in despondent objectless Manhood—Time *objective* and subjective—

(*CN* iii. 4048)

Kathleen Coburn notes that part of this Notebook page has been cut away and speculates that it could have contained 'Time, Real and Imaginary'. Yet although there are obviously some elements common to this Notebook entry and both versions of the poem, including the ostrich simile, there are equally important differences. What the Notebook entry gives us is another, though perhaps related, set of antitheses.

	Sister	Brother
MS	Hope	Time
SL Preface	Schoolboy's daydream	Schoolboy in school
SL	Time Imaginary	Time Real
NB	Time felt in active youth	Time experienced in despondent manhood

It can be seen that these pairs do not quite pair, and that each of them is in fact a different, however related, pairing. Other Notebook passages that have been brought in as comparisons only further complicate the matter. For example, in *CN* iv. 5091, Coleridge writes of Innocence, 'still travelling Eastward, and Memory is the Shade, she casts behind— | While Hope, a singing Pilgrim with girded Loin still westward throws her shade before.' But these lines of 1823 have more to do with 'Youth and Age', about to be written (see Ch. 3), than with 'Time, Real and Imaginary', though they do show the continuity of Coleridge's interest in the subject.

It is possible to find philosophical suggestions in the two figures, as does Edward Kessler, who argues that the sister suggests *natura naturata*:

her retrospective vision can only comprehend things made, not things in the making. By only looking backward, potential power from within is thwarted and life becomes a series of completed but discontinuous moments. With her face reverted, the girl seems to be trapped by the phantoms of time and space, by appearances, and by her own physical senses: she 'looks' and 'listens' for what is past. . . . If she is supposed to embody 'Time real,' she represents a partial conception of reality despite her human sympathy for her brother. She seems to lack a guiding 'idea' of Hope that eventually provides her brother with his goal, even when that goal cannot be verified by the senses.

The boy is accordingly regarded as *natura naturans*: 'he resembles the ever-seeking poet, who uses his imagination to create a "reality" that the backward-looking understanding cannot conceive of.'[44] In this interpretation, Coleridge's own identification of the girl with Hope (and, presumably, with Time Imaginary) is deliberately disregarded. A more fruitful approach might be to take up James Dykes Campbell's intriguing suggestion of 1893: that the poem has something to do with Coleridge's sister. Anne Coleridge (1767–91) was some four years older than Samuel. His earliest extant letter, written to his mother from Christ's Hospital, mentions her beauty (4 February 1785, *CL* i. 1), and during her final illness he wrote an anguished poem, 'On Receiving an Account that His Only Sister's Death was Inevitable'. Verses sent to Charles Lamb express how important she had been to him:

> On her soft Bosom I repos'd my cares
> And gain'd for every wound an healing Tear
> To her I pour'd forth all my puny Sorrows,
> (As a sick patient in his Nurse's arms)
> And of the Heart those hidden Maladies
> That shrink asham'd from even Friendship's Eye.
> (29 December 1794, *CL* i. 147)

A touching memory of their play together occurs in 'Frost At Midnight', ll. 42–3: 'sister more beloved, | My playmate when we both were clothed alike!' The suggestion that the germ of the poem lies in a game between the two during a visit home from Christ's Hospital is a convincing one. (What did they devise to make those ostrich-like pinions?) In their race, Anne, being older, 'Far outstripp'd' him, but she looked back with concern for her laggard brother. For his part, the poet in him perceived himself, running regularly but slowly, as an image of 'real'—or as we might say, clock—Time; while she in her freedom of movement became imaginary Time or, alternatively, a figure of Hope. In later Notebook entries he would move further from the remembered scene to speculations that were less closely related to this poem than to later ones, but that nevertheless retained links among them.

---

[44] *Coleridge's Metaphors of Being* (Princeton, NJ: Princeton University Press, 1979), 86–7.

'To Two Sisters' and 'The Visionary Hope'

'Hope and Time' and 'To William Wordsworth' have in common the allegorization of Hope. Indeed, Hope has become the dominant poetic theme of this phase of the poet's life. In 'To Two Sisters', written in 1807 and published in *The Courier* on 10 December of that year, the theme reappears in connection with the poet's friendship with Mary Morgan and Charlotte Brent, wife and sister-in-law of his friend J. J. Morgan. Coleridge's tone toward the sisters is brotherly, yet he must have recognized some other than brotherly feeling for Charlotte Brent when, noting her twenty-fourth birthday on 5 November 1807, he added that the letters of her name 'make the words *Batchelor t'enter*'.[45] Sentimental idealization mingles with a faint fragrance of the erotic in this poem, and there is at the same time a certain indistinctness, as if one woman friend or love object could easily be confused with another. This very indistinctness and confusion becomes a subject of this poem.

> Sisters, like you, with more than sisters' love;
> So like you *they*, and so in *you* were seen
> Their relative statures, tempers, looks and mien,
> That oft, dear ladies! you have been to me
> At once a vision and reality.
>
> (*Poems*, 410)

The sisters that he sees behind and through (l. 35) these two can be none other than Sara and Mary Hutchinson, and his fantasy of both pairs of sisters 'placed around one hearth' recalls the sites of two poems of 1802. In the 'Letter to Sara Hutchinson' he had written:

> It was as calm as this, that happy night
> When Mary, thou, & I together were,
> The low-decaying Fire our only light,
> And listen'd to the Stillness of the Air!
> (*Poems*, 354, ll. 99–102)

The same scene appears in the beautiful and moving lyric, 'A Day-Dream':

> . . . in one quiet room we three are still together.
>
> The shadows dance upon the wall,
> By the still dancing fire-flames made . . .
> (*CPW* i. 385)

---

[45] (*CN* ii. 3186). Coburn's note suggests that talk with Charlotte Brent 'was freer and more flippant than the serious talk of Coleridge's circles heretofore, and perhaps was sought at this wretched period for that reason.'

Doubtless because of their personal content, during Coleridge's lifetime the lines from the 'Letter to Sara Hutchinson' remained in manuscript, 'A Day-Dream' was not published until 1828, and only a
truncated version of 'To Two Sisters' appeared in a collected edition,
that of 1834.[46]

Like the extended passage on Hope in 'To William Wordsworth' and
the 'Emblem' of 'Hope and Time', 'To Two Sisters' develops a drama
involving the allegorization of the poet's hope.

> Hope long is dead to me! an orphan's tear
> Love wept despairing o'er his nurse's bier.
> Yet she flutters o'er her grave's green slope:
> For Love's despair is but the ghost of Hope!
>
> (ll. 41–4)

This little drama of mourning prefigures situations in much later
poems such as 'Love's Apparition and Evanishment' (1833), while variants of line 44 recur in a number of other contexts, to be discussed in
connection with 'The Visionary Hope'. Yet the poet's Hope is not
entirely gone, for, stimulated by the sisters, his memories have at least
partially reanimated it—'Hope re-appearing dim in memory's guise'
(1. 20)—and the poem ends on a far more positive note than its subtitle,
'A Wanderer's Farewell', would lead one to expect, with the poet
dreaming of both pairs of sisters in a metaphor that is once more to be
found in later poems: 'Fond recollections all my fond heart's food'.
Although the poet can no longer have the primary experience of love, he
can possess the memory, in this instance the double memory, of it. Yet
in a poem probably written just a few years after 'The Two Sisters', that
sense of balance is gone, and the poet temporarily retreats into solips-
ism and self-pity.

'The Visionary Hope', conjecturally dated 1810,[47] is the last among
the group of poems written prior to the publication of *Sibylline Leaves*,
centring on the allegorization of Hope. This poem takes up the theme
that 'Hope is long dead to me!' in 'To Two Sisters'; but now the poet is
seen in complete isolation (except for the ghost of his own dead Hope)
and further distanced by being presented in the third person. Like
Hamlet's Claudius, he kneels and tries to pray but cannot; unlike
Claudius, however, he does not reveal the cause of his condition.
Outward signs indicate his state of acedia without explaining it:

[46] Entitled 'On Taking Leave of——1817', this version reduced the poem's 52 lines to 13.
The whole poem did not appear in a collected edition until 1877–80. See *CPW* i. 411 n.
[47] *CPW* i. 416; *Poems* 418.

> An alien's restless mood but half concealing,
> The sternness on his gentle brow confessed
> Sickness within and miserable feeling . . .

Yet line 14—'Each night was scattered by its own loud screams'—by echoing the night-screams of 'The Pains of Sleep' (1803) tells us that, like the earlier poem, this one concerns the effects of Coleridge's opium addiction. Where in 'The Pains of Sleep' the poet could at least pray aloud, here he can only lament, and his lament constitutes another narrative of the death of Hope—truly an 'abject' in Rajan's sense.

We have already seen Coleridge's tendency to think in terms of personifications. Nowhere is this illustrated more strongly than in line 20 of 'The Visionary Hope': 'For Love's Despair is but Hope's pining Ghost!' This virtually replicates line 44 of 'To Two Sisters' ('For Love's despair is but the ghost of Hope'), and variants of the line appear in 'Constancy to An Ideal Object' ('Hope and Despair meet in the porch of Death!') and in the version of the prose 'Allegoric Vision' published with *A Lay Sermon* in 1817 ('Like two strangers that have fled to the same shelter from the same storm, not seldom do Despair and Hope meet for the first time in the porch of Death!').[48] Yet the insight that despair and hope are not opposites but are, rather, interrelated does not strengthen the poet in 'The Visionary Hope'. Instead, the poem reaches a dead end with the thought that although the power of hope, or at least of his hope, is illusory, he would rather live with that illusion than with the reality of its absence. Coleridge was to address the theme of Hope with poetic success again; but for the time being it had run its course.

* * *

At the conclusion of *The Prelude* Wordsworth projects a joint enterprise for himself and Coleridge:

> Prophets of Nature, we to them will speak
> A lasting inspiration, sanctified
> By reason and by truth; what we have loved
> Others will love; and we will teach them how . . .
>
> (xiii. 442–5)

In 'To William Wordsworth' Coleridge declined this mission. Having shown what he thought was left to him as a poet in the Coleorton poem,

---

[48] *CPW* i. 456, 590. On the dating of 'Constancy to an Ideal Object' see Ch. 4. The 'Allegoric Vision' was first published in 1795 and a later version in *The Courier* for 31 Aug. 1811, but neither of these has the opening passage which first appears in 1817. See *Lay Sermons*, 133.

and having inscribed his early poetic self in the manuscript of 'Hope and Time', he had gone on to produce in 'To Two Sisters' an example of precisely the sort of work one would have expected on the basis of those two texts. With its intimately personal subject matter, its discursive style, and its featuring of personifications in a miniature allegory, 'To Two Sisters' epitomizes Coleridge's later poetry. This is indeed, as Geoffrey Hill says of 'To William Wordsworth', 'a transfiguring of weakness into strength'. However, with 'The Visionary Hope' the theme of Hope in Coleridge's poetry reaches its limit. In order to go beyond it, Coleridge had to recognize and address what had become his only true subject: the abyss within himself.

2 NEGATION

As his greatest poems show, Coleridge always had a darker side to his vision of Being, although it was tempered by his vision of a harmoniously interrelated order of things, as expressed in these famous lines of 'The Eolian Harp' (1795):

> And what if all of animated nature
> Be but organic Harps diversely fram'd,
> That tremble into thought, as o'er them sweeps
> Plastic and vast, one intellectual breeze,
> At once the Soul of each, and God of all?
> (*CPW* i. 102)

In the years after Coleridge's return from Malta the wholeness of this vision is lost; and one of the most memorable expressions of this loss is part of a Notebook passage of 1807. The passage comprises 41 lines (not counting those scored out), beginning as prose or very free verse and culminating in 11 lines of blank verse. At the end Coleridge wrote, '(I wrote these Lines, as an imitation of Du Bartas, as translated by our Sylvester—).' Perhaps on the supposition that the passage was merely an imitation, this material remained unpublished until 1912, when E. H. Coleridge printed the last 11 lines under the bracketed heading 'Coeli Enarrant'.[1] The reference to the first line of Psalm 19 ('The heavens declare the glory of God; and the firmament sheweth his handywork') may seem portentously ironic, but there seems no alternative to using it as a title at this point. The lines themselves form a memorable statement that adumbrates the disjunctive world of the poems Coleridge was to write a few years later.

[*'Coeli Enarrant'*]

The Notebook entry begins with imagery of fire and the web of Time, a web which at first provides support for the poet's vivid dream of

---

[1] *CPW* i. 486. E. H. Coleridge evidently did not have access to the Notebook passage but instead printed the text 'from an MS of uncertain date' which he conjectured to be 1830. My text here is that of Notebook 19, BL Add MS 47, 516, ff. 12v–13r. *Cf. CN* ii. 3107.

happy infantile dependence, expressed in one of Coleridge's favourite images—the Babe nursing at its mother's breast. A unity like that of 'The Eolian Harp' passage is temporarily established:

> Life wakeful over all knew no gradation
> That Bliss in its excess became a Dream;
> For every sense, each thought & each sensation
> Lived in my eye, transfigured ~~yet~~ not suprest.

Then something sinister happens. The web of time becomes not supportive but entrapping, and the poet finds himself in a universe of perpetually deferred gratification: 'What never is but only is to be | This is not Life—'. After two lines of exclamatory protest, he breaks off and starts again, this time with the image of a dark sun and starless sky. Then, after cancelling the new passage he writes out the poem now known as 'Coeli Enarrant'.

The long hiatus between composition and publication may have resulted from editors' taking too literally Coleridge's note about 'an imitation of Du Bartas'. Actually, a comparison of 'Coeli Enarrant' with the Du Bartas/Sylvester *Divine Weeks* shows the latter to be less of a source than a counter-text presenting generally accepted Renaissance ideas about the universe that are explicitly rejected in Coleridge's poem. The imagery of stars in the night sky with which Coleridge begins may be contrasted with *Divine Weeks* i. 42: 'By th'ordered Daunce unto the Starres assign'd'[2]—which turns out to be the opposite in 'Coeli Enarrant'—and to 592 'those bright Spangles that the Heav'ns adorne'—which is hardly like Coleridge's sinister 'conven'd conspiracy of spies'. The traditional idea of the world as a book written by God for us to read appears in Du Bartas/Sylvester, ll. 174–6:

> The World's a Booke in *Folio*, printed all
> With God's great Workes in Letters Capitall:
> Each Creature, is a Page, and each effect,
> A fair Caracter, void of all defect.

This idea is, again, countered by Coleridge:

> . . . all is blank on high,
> No constellations alphabet the Sky—
> The Heavens one large black letter only shews.

> (5–7)

---

[2] Quotations from the *Divine Weeks* refer to *The Divine Weeks and Works of Guillaume De Saluste Sieur Du Bartas*, transl. by Josuah Sylvester, ed. Susan Snyder (Oxford: Clarendon Press 1979), i. 'The First Day of the First Weeke', 111–34.

Imagery of Night and darkness appear in both texts, but once more to opposite ends. In *Divine Weeks*, i. 406–8:

> . . . groapingly yee seek
> In nights blacke darknes for the secret things
> Seal'd in the Casket of the King of Kings

There follows the analogy of the

> finall *Calendar*,
> Where, in *Red letters* (not with us frequented)
> The certain Date of that *Great Day* is printed.
>   (412–14)

Coleridge's opposite point is that the universe, as manifested by the black sky, is unreadable, indecipherable. Although *Divine Weeks* does describe Chaos, it is only as a prelude to the Creation:

> The dreadful Darknes of the *Memphytistes./*
> The sad blacke horror of *Cimerian* mistes,
> The sable fumes of Hells infernal vault
> (Or if ought darker in the World be thought)
> Muffled the face of that profound Abisse[3]

In contrast Coleridge's poem proceeds *towards* nothingness in its surprising climactic trope of the world as a schoolboy being beaten for not getting his reading lesson right.

In printing 'Coeli Enarrant', E. H. Coleridge astutely noted an anecdote of Christ's Hospital in Leigh Hunt's autobiography, in which a child is slapped by James Boyer during a reading lesson. Boyer was in fact a notorious flogging master.[4] Although Coleridge claimed to have been beaten by him only once and to have had one other narrow escape (*TT* i. 327, 144), he must have witnessed other beatings: he remembered this aspect of Boyer well, and referred to it a number of times in later years. In his Marginalia to Richard Baxter's *Reliquiae Baxterianae* (copy B), Coleridge notes: ' "Nihil in intellectu quod non prius in sensu", my old Master, Rd J. Boyer, the Hercules Furens of the phlogistic Sect, but else an incomparable Teacher, used to translate—first reciting the Latin words & observing that they were the fundamental article of the Peripatetic School—"You must flog a boy before you can

---

[3] ll. 301–5. Snyder ii. 770, notes that 301 refers to the 9th plague of Egypt (palpable darkness) in Exod. 10: 21–3, and that in the *Odyssey*, ix. 13–15, the sun never shone in the land of the Cimmerii, far to the west.

[4] *CPW* i. 486 n. See *The Autobiography of Leigh Hunt*, ed. J. E. Morpurgo (London: Cresset Press, 1948), 74.

make him understand"—or "You must lay it in at the Tail before you get it into the Head.["]' (*CM* i. 354); one can well imagine that the beaten schoolboy in the poem is based on a childhood recollection of Christ's Hospital. The black-letter text that the boy is given to read may, as Kathleen Coburn suggests (*CN* ii. 3107), reflect some lines in Richard Crashaw's 'In the Glorious Epiphany of Our Lord'; but, if so, it does so once more as a counter-text. 'And as a large black letter', Crashaw wrote, 'Use to spell thy beauties better, | And make the night itself their torch to thee.' Here, however, the poor student of the simile finds an indecipherable text whose only letter signifies both a cry of pain and absolute nullity—'O!' 'The groaning world', the tenor of this vehicle, is that of Rom. 8: 22, 'For we know that the whole creation groaneth and travaileth in pain until now'; except that the fulfilment of the last two words of Paul's text is absent here.

In presenting Nature as an unreadable text, Coleridge is surely conscious of nullifying the possibility of literary symbolism and with it the notion of the poet as interpreter of the universe. Tim Fulford contrasts 'the beneficent teaching of nature's "eternal language" in "Frost At Midnight" '[5]; and we may also think of the Coleridge's quest for a symbolic language of Nature in a celebrated Notebook entry:

In looking at objects of Nature while I am thinking, as at yonder moon dim-glimmering thro' the dewy window-pane, I seem rather to be seeking, as it were *asking*, a symbolical language for something within me that already and forever exists, than observing any thing new. Even when that latter is the case, yet still I have always an obscure feeling as if that new phaenomenon were the dim Awaking of a forgotten or hidden Truth of my inner nature/ It is still interesting as a Word, a Symbol! It is [Gr.] *Logos*, the Creator! <and the Evolver!>

(*CN* ii. 2546)

The unreadable world of 'Coeli Enarrant', in contrast, has no place in it for the oracular poet, bearer of the incarnate Word. In the poetry of such a world the appropriate tropes are the most conscious ones—simile rather than metaphor, personification rather than synecdoche; the mode of signification is typically allegory rather than symbolism; and the most characteristic strategy is calling attention to its own fictiveness lest the reader take it for what it is not: an attempt to re-create the 'high' Romantic mode. This is also the world that Coleridge would create in a powerful work of 1811, a composition largely known, like 'Coeli Enarrant', in the form of editorially arranged fragments: 'Limbo' and 'Ne Plus Ultra'.

<hr />

[5] *Coleridge's Figurative Language* (Basingstoke and London, 1991), 82.

The 'Limbo' Constellation

In April and May of 1811 Samuel Taylor Coleridge was at one of the lowest points of what had become a tormented personal life. The traumatic rupture with Wordsworth had occurred less than six months before. In February his old friend George Burnett, also an opium addict, had died in miserable circumstances; and the shock of Burnett's death had driven Coleridge's friend, Mary Lamb, into one of her periods of insanity. Coleridge's own dependence on laudanum had increased to a frightening extent. Some of the time he lived with his friends John and Mary Morgan and Charlotte Brent in Hammersmith, sometimes in lodgings at Southampton Buildings in Chancery Lane. A pattern had developed in which he would quarrel with the Morgans about his addiction or its effects, remove to Southampton Buildings, become terrified by his inability to control his drug habit, write abject apologies for his behaviour to the Morgans, and move back to Hammersmith. Most of the poetry he wrote in this period was in his Notebooks, and it was there that he produced one of his most remarkable literary works, dealing with his feeling of inner vastation. As this composite text lacks even a name, though names have been given to parts of it, a description of its parts and a summary of its publication history are necessary before it is considered it is detail.

The poems known as 'Limbo' and 'Ne Plus Ultra' are part of a longer piece of prose and verse in Coleridge Notebook 18.[6] In 1818 Coleridge printed five lines of this material in *The Friend* (i. 494 n.) under the title 'Moles'. He seems to have made no effort to publish any of the rest until in September 1828 he revised part of it into a poem intended for his friend Alaric Watts's annual *The Literary Souvenir*, describing it to Watts as 'a pretended Fragment of Lee, the Tragic Poet, containing a description of Limbo, & according to my own fancy containing some of the most forcible Lines & with the most original imagery that my niggard Muse ever made me a present of—' (Letter dated 14 September 1828, *CL* vi. 758). The pseudo-ascription to Lee, who had been confined for insanity from 1684 to 1689, would have alerted Watts to the phantasmagoric nature of the poem. (Such an ascription may have been something of a convention; compare Blake's denigration of 'a

---

[6] BL Add. MS 47515. The following discussion of the manuscript is based upon my own examination of Notebook 18 at the Department of Manuscripts, BL, compared with the text and notes published by Kathleen Coburn in *CN* iii. 4073–4, and the text and apparatus prepared by Professor J. C. C. Mays for the *Collected Coleridge* edition of Coleridge's poetry. I am grateful to Professor Mays for allowing me to consult this material in typescript.

Poem signed with the name of Nat Lee which perhaps he never wrote & perhaps he wrote in a paroxysm of insanity'[7] and Coleridge's own copying six lines of nonsense verse into a notebook [*CN* iv. 4931] and ascribing them to Lee.) However, Watts did not receive the manuscript that Coleridge thought he had left at the editor's doorstep, and the best Coleridge could do was to send twenty lines of fair copy later. As for the rest, he explained, 'A rude Copy, I have—but in transcribing it for you I had made numerous alterations, and large additions, written more meo on sundry Scraps of Paper—which are either destroyed or in terra incognita.' (Letter conjecturally dated December 1828, *CL* vi. 779.) There the matter rested until the so-called 'deathbed edition' of the *Poetical Works* of 1834.

As is widely known, the editor of the 1834 edition, Henry Nelson Coleridge, necessarily had to make decisions that would otherwise have been the poet's. H. N. Coleridge printed twenty-seven lines of verse for the first time under the title 'Limbo', reprinted the 5-line 'Moles' from *The Friend* (with variants), and printed, again for the first time, the 21 line 'Ne Plus Ultra'—a title that may very well not have been S. T. Coleridge's. In the 1893 *Poetical Works* edited by James Dykes Campbell, a 38-line 'Limbo' was presented along with 'Ne Plus Ultra'. This procedure was repeated in 1912 by E. H. Coleridge, who also included some variants from Notebook 18 and others from a manuscript now in the Humanities Research Center of the University of Texas. The 1912 edition also gave the reader, for the first time, twelve lines under the title 'On Donne's Poem "To a Flea," ' correctly dating it 1811, but placing in Volume ii, with 'Limbo' (dated 1817) and 'Ne Plus Ultra' (dated 1826) in Volume i. Thus was obscured the identity of these as parts of a single text, other parts of which had not been published at all.

What all this demonstrates is that, although Coleridge may well have worked up a poem for Alaric Watts using the material in his Notebook, no such poem is now known to exist, and the only authoritative source for the text under discussion is Coleridge's Notebook draft, supplemented by the fragmentary MS from Sara Coleridge's album that E. H. Coleridge termed '*MS. S. T. C.*' Any other rendition, from Henry Nelson Coleridge's on, lacks the authority of the poet. It should be noted that excising parts of the manuscript entails other than theoretical difficulties. Line 2 of 'Limbo' as rendered by Campbell, E. H. Coleridge, and subsequent editors reads 'It frightens Ghosts, as here Ghosts

---

[7] 'Public Address', *The Poetry and Prose of William Blake*, ed. David V. Erdman (Garden City, New York: Doubleday, 1970) 581.

frighten Men'. However, there is no antecedent to which 'It' can refer, since 'It' is the flea that E. H. Coleridge relegated to Volume ii. That same flea is the subject of the verbs 'cross'd', 'Be pulveris'd', 'given', and 'shrinks' in the four lines following. These lines simply cannot be understood without the lines that Coleridge entitled 'On Donne's first Poem', and the failure to understand them has resulted in some surprising explications, which our present knowledge of the circumstances of composition should enable us to avoid.

The text at hand comprises a piece of untitled prose that breaks into some dozen lines (some scored out) of verse, which in turn are interrupted by the only title that appears in the whole: 'On Donne's first Poem'. Verse then continues, to be broken only by a single sentence of prose after the line that we know as the last of 'Limbo'. On a new page, after one line related to 'Limbo', there follows, without a title, the poem we know as 'Ne Plus Ultra', written out cleanly and with a finer pen than most of what precedes it. Some other physical details of the Notebook manuscript will bear comment later. At this point, and before considering the text in detail, three more general aspects of Coleridge should be considered: his interest in theology and theosophy, his sense of the phantasmagoric, and his engagement with the poetry of John Donne.

The Limbo constellation, as I shall term the entire text, obviously uses conceptions and terms drawn from Coleridge's theological and theosophical interests. Perhaps the strongest single influence here is Jakob Boehme, and some close connections between parts of this text and some passages in Boehme's writings, especially with the thirty-fourth of Boehme's *Forty Questions Concerning the Soul* ('What is the miserable and horrible condition of the Damned Souls?') have been demonstrated.[8] Such parallels enrich our appreciation of the rich allusiveness of the text[9] and therefore help us to engage with it fully, as long as we do not mistake it for an exposition of theology or philosophy. Most of it is indeed characterized by verbal playfulness, and terms such as Limbo, Hell, and Purgatory are used with deliberate fuzziness. Only the last part, the twenty-one lines of verse now known as 'Ne Plus Ultra', centres seriously on a theological subject—the existence of evil—and here whatever sources there may be are fully assimilated to Coleridge's own purposes. The text throughout is marked by a sense of

[8] George F. Ridenour, 'Source and Allusion in Some Poems of Coleridge', *Studies in Philology*, 60 (1963), 187–95.

[9] See Frederick Burwick, who also adduces some allusions to Jean Paul Richter: 'Coleridge's "Limbo" and "Ne Plus Ultra": The Multeity of Intertextuality', *Romanticism Past and Present*, 9 (1985), 35–45.

the phantasmagoric, and the tone deeply coloured by a Coleridgean version of Metaphysical wit.

Coleridge's sensibility had always been attracted by phantasmagoria, as attested by a poem like 'The Nose', written in 1789.[10] Although no one has suggested that 'The Nose' is a sustained religious allegory, parts of it, for example 'Like Phlegethon in waves of fire my verse shall flow!' (10) are reminiscent of 'Limbo'. Other parts are likewise reminiscent of Donne; line 25, 'Shorn of thy rays thou shott'st a fearful gleam' is virtually an allusion to 'A Nocturnall Upon S. Lucies Day', which is also echoed in 'Limbo'. 'The Nose', which Coleridge ironically called 'An Odaic Rhapsody', aims at the comic grotesque, but Coleridge could also delight in phantasmagoria for its own sake. Twice in his Notebooks he copied out nonsense verses which in *CN* iv. 4931 he pretended, once more reminding us of 'Limbo', were 'Lee's rapturous lines':

> O that my Mouth could bleat like butter'd Peas
> Engendering Windmills in the Northern s[eas]
> Coaches & Waggons rumble down my Nose,
> And blue iniquity flow off in pro~~p~~se—
> Then run full tilt at your Subjunctive Mood,
> And fatten Padlocks on Antarctic Food—[11]

This passage, with some substantial variants, is part of a poem that has since been published as an anonymous lyric of 1617[12]; the substantial variants may or may not be Coleridge's own, but what is germane in both instances is Coleridge's sense of word-play and his delight in the grotesque, both of which are amply illustrated in the Limbo constellation.

That Coleridge had a special interest in Donne is evident throughout his career, but certain aspects of that interest are especially germane here. Coleridge probably first read Donne in 1796,[13] and at that time he proposed to write 'Satires in the manner of Donne' (*CN* i. 171). His celebrated epigram, 'On Donne's Poetry', usually dated *c*. 1818, may have been written in another form as early as 1798.[14] In 1799 he credited his

---

[10] *CPW* i. 8–9; ll. 11–20 were first published in 1798, the rest in the *Poetical Works* of 1834.

[11] Coburn notes that in *CN* iii. 4072 *n* the 6 lines are quoted with variants from the Ottery Copy Book (Victoria College Library).

[12] *A Nonsense Anthology*, ed. Carolyn Wells (New York, 1902), 16–17. The poem also appears in *The Faber Book of Comic Verse*, ed. Michael Roberts (London: Faber & Faber, 1942), 1.

[13] See George Whalley, 'The Harvest on the Ground', *University of Toronto Quarterly*, 39 (1969), 263. Whalley identifies the edition Coleridge read as Anderson's *British Poets: The Poetical Works of John Donne* (Edinburgh: Mundell and Son, 1793; bound as vol. iv of *A Complete Edition of the Poets of Great Britain*).

[14] See Mary Lynn Johnson, 'How Rare is a "Unique Annotated Copy" of Coleridge's *Sibylline Leaves*?' *BNYPL* 76 (1975), 476.

reading of Donne with his outgrowing the earlier influences of Gray and Collins. 'From this cause it is,' he wrote, 'that what *I* call metaphysical Poetry gives me so much delight' (*CN* i. 383). By underscoring 'I', Coleridge dramatized the difference between his use of the term and Dr Johnson's condescending one. In addition to the peculiar importance Donne held for Coleridge is the fact that what Coleridge appreciated in Donne strikingly anticipates the critics who rediscovered him early in the twentieth century, as this later note demonstrates:

Wonder-exciting vigour, intenseness and peculiarity of thought, using at will the almost boundless stores of a capacious memory, and exercised on subjects, where we have no right to expect it—this is the wit of Donne!

(*CM* ii. 17)

In 1811 Coleridge was preparing a series of lectures that would include Donne, and he borrowed for the purpose Charles Lamb's copy of the 1669 edition of Donne's *Poems* (now in the Beinecke Library, Yale University), which he richly annotated. As George Whalley remarks, 'When he began to annotate Lamb's copy of the *Poems* in 1811, he brought to it some years of enthusiastic critical reflection, the experience of attempted imitation, and an exceptionally fine ear' (*CM* ii. 213). His response to Donne in turn permeated the satire on false wit that he was writing, to the extent that it transformed itself from prose into verse, five lines of which he inscribed in revised form in Lamb's copy (*CM* ii. 217 n.), sealing, as it were, a link with the text before us.[15]

The Notebook entry begins as satiric prose, with a trio of personalities that might serve as the kernels for Theophrastian characters or minor figures in a Restoration comedy: Crathmocraulo, Tungstic Acid, and Copioso. Of these, Tungstic Acid has been identified by Coburn as Charles Lamb on the basis of an earlier Notebook entry (*CN* i. 977 and n.), but the identities of these figures is less important than the play of fantasy with which they are presented. The common denominator is Coleridge's linking of false wit with vermin. '*Crathmocraulo's* Thoughts like Lice,' he begins. (He liked this made-up name so well he used it or variations of it later in different contexts. For example, in a letter to the Morgans dated 11 February 1812, he writes of two lice that he found on

---

[15] 'On Donne's first Poem':

> Be proud, as Spaniards. Leap for Pride, ye Fleas!
> In Nature's *minim* Realm ye're now Grandees.
> Skip-jacks no more, nor civiller Skip-Johns.
> Thrice-honor'd Fleas! I greet you all, as *Dons*.
> In Phoebus' Archives register'd are ye.
> And this your Patent of Nobility!

his neck during a coach trip: 'The larger of the two was called
SCRUMBOCREEP, the other SCLAWMICRAWLO', and this leads to a comic
dream of hell followed by a pun on '*license*'.[16]) This yoking leads to an
idea that will shortly become much more important. Tungstic Acid's
wit is 'of the Flea kind' and his jokes 'Flea-skips & Flea-bites'. Prose becomes inadequate for the play of Coleridge's imagination, and he
breaks into verse, scores out his first lines, begins again, producing a
brilliant image that is the first to indicate that something more than
banter is being produced: 'The poor <dead> Jests, like Gudgeons
drugg'd and drown'd, | Float wrong side up, in a full Flow of Dribble.'
This discharge of wit leads, after two more lines, to thoughts of Donne
and specifically, after the 'Flea-skips & Flea-bites' of Tungstic Acid's
wit, to Donne's 'The Flea', which came first in the edition of Donne
that Coleridge was reading in the spring of 1811. At this point Coleridge
wrote out the only title that appears in the entire text—'On Donne's
first Poem'—and began again. The couplets that follow begin as a
celebration of fleas—'No Skip-Jacks now' because 'skipjack' has among
its meanings 'a pert, shallow-brained fellow' and 'hopping, skipping,
jumping' (*OED*, *s.v.*).[17] These fleas have advanced to noble status,
being, in an awful pun, 'Descendants from a noble Race of *Dons*'. At this
point the poem is a *jeu d'esprit* combining the satirical elements of the
prose prologue with an ironic style derived from Donne himself.

    Following a space, a second group of couplets begins to mythologize
the subject as 'that great ancestral Flea'; and here begin the theological
metaphors that characterize the rest of this part of the text. I say 'theological metaphors' because the lines that follow can hardly be read as a
versification of Coleridge's own religious belief. On the contrary, we
can feel his own conviction in his 'Epitaph of the Present Year in the
Monument of Thomas Fuller' (*CPW* ii. 975), dated 28 November 1833:
'A Lutheran stout, I hold for Goose-and Gaundry | Both the Pope's
Limbo and his fiery Laundry'. And how little he cared about theological distinctions can be seen in part of what he inscribed preceding a

---

[16] *CL* iii. 369. *Cf.* also Coleridge's letter to Charlotte Brent dated 20 Nov. 1813: 'The longer
I live, the more do I loathe in stomach, & deprecate in Judgment, all, *all* Bluestockingism. The
least possible of it implies at least two *Nits*, in one egg a male, in t'other a female—& if not
killed. *O the sense of the Lady will be Lic*ense! Crathmo-crawlo!—' (*CL* iii. 905). There is a curious resemblance between wordplay such as this and the made-up language of Sara Fricker
Coleridge, the 'Lingo Grande' discussed by Molly Lefebure in *The Bondage of Love* (London:
Gollancz, 1986), 221–2.
[17] Coburn (*CN* iii. 4104 n.) calls attention to a Notebook reference to Dr Johnson
Coleridge made not long after this: 'a notable Flea-skip for so great a being', possibly referring
to Johnson's remark to Boswell 'Sir, there is no point in settling the point of precedency between a louse and a flea'.

partial version of 'Limbo' in Sara Coleridge's Album in 1827: 'from a dream of Purgatory, alias Limbo' (*CPW* i. 429 n.). In the text at hand the great ancestral Flea's earthly spots have been bleached 'as Papists gloze | In purgatory fire on Bardolph's nose'. This brings in hell as well as Purgatory, for the allusion is to Falstaff's words to Bardolph in *Henry IV, Part I*: 'I never see thy face but I think upon hell-fire, and Dives that lived in purple; for there he is in his robes, burning, burning' (III. i. 31–4). This multiple allusion brings us to Luke 16, not only because Dives is there 'tormented in flame' (24), but for two other reasons. The ancestral flea with its 'earthly spots' is analogous to 'Lazarus . . . full of sores' (20); and the spatial relations adumbrated by father Abraham in the parable are proleptic of those that Coleridge's poem is about to explore: 'Between us and you there is a great gulf fixed: so that they which would pass hence to you cannot; neither can they pass to us, that *would come* from thence' (26). The flea's journey and its consequences will reveal states of spiritual being, but to judge these lines according to some standard of theological correctness[18] is to demand something that they were never meant to offer.

The subject of 'Limbo' has been aptly defined as the crossing of a threshold,[19] and here is where the threshold is found. The ancestral Flea, or perhaps his 'bladdery hide' (like the preserved crocodiles that traditionally hung from the ceilings of apothecary's shops) 'crossed unchang'd and still keeps in ghost-Light | Of lank Half-nothings his, the thinnest Sprite'. We are now at the point where 'Limbo' begins in the published editions, but later in his Notebook Coleridge attempted an alternate, expanded transition of six lines.[20] Here the Flea, 'skimming in the wake' of Charon's boat, gets across the rivers of the underworld without paying the traditional boatman's farthing, and so incurs the kind of wrathful frown that Charon gave the Ithacan beggar, Irus. Irus was a bully and a coward as well in *The Odyssey*; although Odysseus gave him a beating in Ithaca, there is no mention of Irus's death there— but Irus is just the sort of fellow who would have attempted to cheat Charon. (In a fable in *The Friend* for 11 January 1810 [ii. 363–5]

---

[18] See James D. Boulger, *Coleridge As Religious Thinker* (New Haven, 1961), 202. Boulger realizes this poetry is 'not to be taken in a fully serious way', but this appears to diminish it in his view.

[19] Angus Fletcher, ' "Positive Negation": Threshold, Sequence, and Personification in Coleridge', *New Perspectives on Coleridge and Wordsworth*, ed. Geoffrey Hartman (New York: Columbia University Press, 1972), 141.

[20] Coburn, *CN* 4073 n.; Mays, apparatus to the forthcoming *Poetical Works* in the *Collected Coleridge*. Coburn also compares 'Puriphlegothon Cocytus' to 'Phlegothon's rage, Cocytus' wailings hoarse' in *Fragment of an Ode on Napoleon* (*CPW* ii. 1003).

Coleridge used Irus as a stand-in for Napoleon.) This passage ends with 'Unchang'd it cross'd & shall, & c', bringing us back to the line that ends 'and still keeps in ghost-Light'. This alternative transition introduces classical elements that further remove the passage from theological territory, make the imagery even more grotesque by making the inflated skin that of the Doctor or Druggist (the druggist who supplied Coleridge with laudanum?) himself, and intensify the comedy element by rhyming 'Cocytus' with 'fright us'. Here is where, by either route, we enter Limbo.

The figure that we might by now aptly compare with Blake's Visionary Head of the Ghost of a Flea is now 'Of lank Half-nothings his, the thinnest Sprite'. The thinness of the occupants of this mental space calls attention to one of its its salient characteristics: two-dimensionality. Michael Cooke aptly refers to 'the hypostasis of terrifying space' here.[21] The personification of Space itself is 'Lank'. On the threshold of nonbeing, these 'Ghosts' are terrified by their visitant from outside: 'The sole true ~~Any~~ *Something* this is Limbo Den | It frights Ghosts as Ghosts here frighten men'. In 1820 Coleridge rewrote these two lines in the context of a discussion of metaphysics: 'And guests unwelcome to their shadowy den | That frightens Ghosts as Ghosts here frighten men!' (*CN* iv. 4692). Here the lines illustrate the statement 'to Dreamers, an empty sound to the Blind, an Apparition in the Limbo of Modern Psilosophy, an alien Substance'. Coleridge elsewhere derived *Psilosophy* 'from the Greek, psilos slender, and Sophia Wisdom, in opposition to Philosophy, the love of Wisdom and the Wisdom of Love' (Letter to J. H. Bohte dated 27 February 1819, *CL* iv. 922). This 'mechanical atomistic Psilosophy', as he called it in *The Friend* (i. 94 n.), is contrasted to a visionary power that the Notebook passage goes on to invoke:

if only the souls of better mould, made to live in the courts of the Sun, could be ~~drawn~~ called into the Valley of Vision—if only I could raise *them* by magnetic power from their present twilight of Somnambulism to Clairvoyance—what a new Heaven & a new Earth, would begin to reveal itself.

What this statement, with its reference to Rev. 21: 1, shows is how close the conception of the 'Ghosts' trapped in Limbo is to the apocalyptic—and yet how far. Just as the 'If' clause above will never be realized, so the 'Ghosts' await their own destruction, which is a travesty of the apocalyptic, not to be followed by their being made to live in the courts of the sun.

[21] 'The Manipulation of Space in Coleridge's Poetry', *New Perspectives on Coleridge and Wordsworth*, 177.

> Thence cross unraz'd and shall, ~~at~~ some ~~dire~~ Hour,
> Be pulveriz'd by Demogorgon's Power
> And given as poison, to annihilate Souls—

The imagining of Demogorgon seems to involve an apocalyptic moment. As John A. Hodgson remarks, 'The coming of Demogorgon represents a classical version of the Second Coming, the end of time.'[22] However, in this ironical context, the invoking of Demogorgon becomes an example of what I have elsewhere termed Coleridge's 'apocalyptic grotesque' mode, where the sublime is exaggerated to the point of caricature.[23] The 'poison' derived from the pulverized flea begins to act, shrinking the 'Ghosts' to the state described in the passage that Coleridge published, with variants, as 'Moles'.

The mole is another of those images that Coleridge used with special significance. In 'Lines Suggested by the Last Words of Berengarius' (1826), the theologian ahead of his dark time is addressed as 'Lynx among Moles!' (*CPW* i. 460); but we find Coleridge using the image significantly as early as *The Piccolimini* (1800), where Wallenstein tells Illo:

> Mole-eyed, thou mayest but burrow in the earth,
> Blind as that subterrestial, who with wan,
> Lead-coloured shine lighted thee into life.
>
> (I, xi. *CPW* ii. 629–30)

There is no mole in Schiller's original, and we can see that this trope is on its way to achieving the meaning which Coleridge gave to it in a note to 'Essays on the principles of Method' in *The Friend* (1818), where 'Moles' are linked with 'the partizans of a crass and sensual materialism, the advocates of the Nihil nisis ab extra' (i. 494 n.). These Moles are true adherents of 'Psilosophy', sealed beings who believe nothing except what originates inside themselves, and so in our text are 'live Mandrakes of the ground', the mandrake being, according to mythical natural history, a foetus-shaped plant that screamed when uprooted.[24]

---

[22] 'Coleridge, Puns, and "Donne's First Poem": The Limbo of Rhetoric and the Conception of Wit', *John Donne Journal*, 4 (1985), 192 (181–200). Hodgson (198–9, n. 17) also discusses the alchemical origins of this concept of Demogorgon.

[23] 'Coleridge and the Apocalyptic Grotesque', *Coleridge's Visionary Languages*, ed. Tim Fulford and Morton D. Paley (Woodbridge, Suffolk: D. S. Brewer, 1993), 15–25.

[24] The mandrake's scream occurs in Letter I of *Confessions of an Inquiring Spirit*:

> In darkness there to house unknown,
> Far underground,
> Pierc'd by no sound
> Save as such as live in Fancy's ear alone,
> That listens for the uptorn mandrake's parting groan!

ed. H. St. J. Hart, BD (London: Adam & Charles Black, 1956), 39.

With 'The natural Alien of their negative eye', the theme of Negativity,
implicit throughout 'Limbo', is made explicit, will later dominate the
end of the poem, and will finally become the central subject of 'Ne Plus
Ultra'.

The negative space of Limbo has its antecedent not so much in theological conceptions as in literary tradition. As I. A. Richards suggested,
there is a relationship to the Paradise of Fools in *Paradise Lost* iii.
420–500, and especially:

> . . . all these upwhirled aloft,
> Fly o'er the backside of the World far off
> Into a Limbo large and broad . . .[25]

Another antecedent is the Bosch-like world of Pope's Cave of Spleen,
in Canto IV of *The Rape of the Lock*, a place also peopled by personifications and characterized by grotesque imagery. As created by Coleridge,
Limbo is 'not a Place', though it has to be called so for a want of a better
term (Blake might have called it a State) and it hardly has room for the
personifications of Time and Space, who 'Fetter'd from flight, with
Night-mair sense of Fleeing | Strive for their last crepuscular Half-
Being.' In order to fit in, Space has to be made 'Lank', and Time, having
lost his function, is 'scytheless'. However, this a merely a parody of end-
time, as the allusion to Demogorgon was a parody of apocalypse.

That any signs presented by Time and Space are meaningless is in-
dicated by a trope of of unreadability: 'unmeaning they | As Moonlight
on the Dial of the Day'. It has been observed that Coleridge used this
image elsewhere to denote anyone who fails to read a book in the spirit
in which it was written,[26] but it is important to contextualize this comparison to bring out its full meaning. In annotating the anonymous
Eternal Punishment Proved to Be Not Suffering but Privation (London,
1817; BL C. 126. g. 3), Coleridge sharply criticized the author, whom,
in a note on the flyleaf, he accused of 'gross crass materialism' in con-
founding timelessness with Everlasting Time ('an impossible idea').
Coleridge continued:

There is a state above Time, consequently *timeless* (the only sense, in which
Eternity can be predicated of a finite Being), which state is the greatest Good
that Man can seek to possess; and . . . there is a state below Time & therefore
likewise timeless, which is the direst Evil, that man can [*deletions*] eschew
or suffer. These are contrary states, the first being by our Lord [*deletion*]

---

[25] ll. 411–13; see I. A. Richards, *'Coleridge's Minor Poems': A Lecture . . . Delivered . . . at
Montana State University on April 8, 1960* (Missoula, Mo., 1960) 24.
[26] See Kessler, *Coleridge's Metaphors of Being* (Princeton, NJ, 1979), 105.

designated by the name, Eternal Life—the second Eternal Death. Now
Reason by Common Sense informs us, that the mere Negation of a thing is not
the Contrary of that Thing. The Contrary of Love is Hate; not Indifference.
The Death here threatened must therefore be a positive State. This is all we
know from Scripture; and probably all, that in our present condition we are
capable of knowing.

Coleridge later goes on to consider how we can know the meaning that
Scripture intends, giving as an instance four different Greek versions of
words that Jesus spoke 'in his vernacular language'.

Which am I to take? Or rather is it not evident, that no logical deductions can
be drawn from being read at all must be read in and by the same spirit, as that
by which it was written. Who does not do this reads a dial by moon. shine.[27]

Timelessness exists for Coleridge, but not in the closed world of Limbo.
However, functionless Time is played off against a much more substantial figure who 'looks like human Time' and whose image presents
a problem of signification different from that of 'scytheless Time'.
    Coleridge's description of a blind old man whose moon-like face is
turned toward the moon has engendered vastly differing interpretations. Reeve Parker finds that in this description 'a momentary relent-
ing of the vision of limbo becomes a triumphant encounter, the moon in
the old man and the old man finding in each other a companionable
form'.[28] James Boulger, who considers the old man 'recognizably Coleridge himself', believes he 'embodies both spiritual deprivation and
potential spiritual fulfilment'.[29] Edward Kessler also regards the old
man as a Coleridge-surrogate, but as having achieved inner vision in an
entirely positive way: 'His mind is independent of the phenomenal
world, and his soul is like the one described in the *Biographia Literaria*:
"steady and collected in its pure *Act* of inward adoration to the Great I
AM."'[30] For Frederick Burwick, 'The passage on the blind man be-
neath the moon functions as an epic simile on the "unmeaning" time of
limbo'.[31] Stephen Prickett calls attention to the prominence of the verb
'seems' in the passage, and relates this to the doctrine of the unknow-
ability of things-in-themselves: 'The old man of the poem is Coleridge

    [27] From the bottom margin of p. xii, part of a long note beginning on p. viii. The second
sentence, though incorrect syntactically, is what Coleridge wrote, as are the two full stops in
the third sentence.
    [28] *Coleridge's Meditative Art* (Ithaca, NY, 1975), 242. 'Companionable form' is of course a
reference to 'Frost At Midnight', l. 19.   [29] *Coleridge As Religious Thinker*, 110.
    [30] *Coleridge's Metaphors of Being* 101–2, citing the last sentence of the *Biographia Literaria*.
However, this seemingly very positive interpretation is almost immediately qualified by the
statement that 'the poet withholds his commitment to arrested process or absolute being'
(103).   [31] 'Coleridge's "Limbo" and "Ne Plus Ultra" ', 40.

the pure Kantian philosopher—living in a world that is demonstrably unknowable.'[32]

These are extraordinarily different interpretations, yet each of them connects with something that is actually in the passage. The old man who, significantly is *not* in 'Limbo Den', is indeed 'lovely', with his 'steady look sublime' irradiated by moonlight. Yet his loveliness and apparent sublimity are qualified by his blindness. The blindness of a solitary figure is an image that deeply engaged Coleridge over a long period of time. As we have seen, Time is represented by a blind boy in 'Hope and Time'.[33] The blind Homer is invoked in 'Fancy in Nubibus':

> Or list'ning to the Tide, with closèd sight,
> Be that blind Bard, who on the Chian strand,
> By those deep sounds possess'd with inward Light,
> Beheld the Iliad and the Odyssee
> Rise to the swelling of the voiceful Sea!

> (*CPW* i. 435)

In 'The Blossoming of the Solitary Date-Tree', it is Coleridge himself who is 'Like a blind Arab, that from sleep doth start | In lonesome tent' (*CPW* i. 196) listening for the voice of the beloved; and in 'Love's Apparition and Evanishment', it is once more Coleridge who 'in vacant mood' is 'Like a lone Arab, old and blind' (*CPW* i. 488). The image suggests some radical deficiency, but also an undoubted authenticity, as in the Notebook entry 'Mother listening for the *sound* of a still-born child—blind Arab list'ning in the wilderness' (*CN* i. 1244), and in Coleridge's letter to William Sotheby dated 13 July 1802: 'He [a great poet] must have the *ear* of a wild Arab listening in the silent desert . . . the Touch of a Blind Man feeling the face of a darling Child' (*CL* ii. 810). The blind man, Arab or not, lacks the normal human sensory equipment, but for that very reason is forced to cultivate intensely what means he has of learning about the universe. Carried in one direction, the image of the blind man in 'Limbo' suggests Homer 'inform'd with inward Light'; but this is only one point in a spectrum of possible meanings.

Another aspect of Coleridge's interest in this image, one that can be related to inward light in a different way, is seen in his personal

---

[32] *Coleridge and Wordsworth: The Poetry of Growth* (Cambridge, 1970), 202–2. Walter Jackson Bate also considers the world to be unknowable to the old man: 'with his upturned face, he is as unseeing as a statue, and if he turns his face 'moonward' it is only by chance.' *Coleridge* (London: Weidenfeld & Nicolson, 1969 [1968]), 177.

[33] As noted by Coburn (*CN* iii. 4073 n.), who suggests the poems may be close in date.

observations on two blind friends who fished and coursed together (*CN* i. 572). One of them, John Gough of Kendal, is discussed at length in Coleridge's essay 'The Soul and Its Organs of Sense'. Coleridge is particularly fascinated by the substitution of one sense for another:

As to plants and flowers, the rapidity of his touch appears fully equal to that of sight; and the accuracy greater. Good heavens! it needs only to look at him! . . . Why, his face sees all over! It is all one eye!

Coleridge[34] goes on to declare that the human face 'is the mere stamp, the undisturbed *ectypon*, of his own soul!'[35] and that Gough, a Quaker, represented what Coleridge considered the best aspects of his sect without the worst. *Ectypon* means 'worked in relief' in Greek, and is the source of the English word 'ectype', signifying an impression in a soft substance such as clay or a reproduction as distinguished from its prototype (*OED*, *s.v.*). This characteristic of three-dimensionality is also suggested in the old man—'a statue hath such eyes', in contrast to the 'Ghosts', who are 'lank Half-nothings' approaching two-dimensionality. A curiously similar contrast is made in the fifth Philosophical Lecture, where Coleridge contrasts medieval and high Renaissance art. The former is characterized by 'wiry outlines, surfaces imprisoned in the outlines without depth, without force'. In the paintings of Michelangelo and Raphael, the imprisoned arts are liberated: 'There the mighty spirit coming from within had succeeded in taming the intractable matter and in reducing external form to a symbol of the inward and imaginable beauty.'[36] However, immured in the 'circumambience' of 'Limbo Den', the 'Ghosts' will never attain three-dimensionality.

The relationship, or non-relationship, between the old man and the Ghosts is a contrastive one. The old man is beautiful, bathed in light, and at first reassuring in his solidity and his suggestion of an inner life. Yet there are significant ambiguities. His blindness cuts him off from human contact, and the emphasis is, as Prickett observes, on seeming: 'looks like', 'As 'twere', 'seemeth to rejoice', 'seems to gaze at that which seems to gaze on him'. This is surprising because we would expect this 'lovely' sight to suggest *being*, not seeming. This old man might seem like a traditional emblem of Time, were it not for a deliberate difference: 'with fore-top bald & high', he presents no forelock to be

---

[34] Robert Southey and S. T. Coleridge, *Omniana* (London, 1812) ii. 17. The ellipsis is Coleridge's. Kessler, in *Coleridge's Metaphors of Being*, 102, quotes a somewhat differently worded account from H. N. Coleridge's edition of *Literary Remains*.

[35] *Omniana* ii. 18.   [36] *Philosophical Lectures*, 193.

advantageously seized. Furthermore, if we think of the uniquivocally positive implications of moonlight in poems like 'Frost at Midnight' and 'The Rhyme of the Ancient Mariner', where under the transformative power of the moon all things are seen as connected by the principle of the One Life, a further disjunction arises. In this later poem the connections established by the moon are consciously fictive similitudes rather than being indicative of any reality. The old man remains in a separate space, admired by the poet in passing, but inaccessible to the 'Ghosts' or anyone else—a glorious irrelevancy.

Now Coleridge's text returns to Limbo itself. In what seems to be a first try at the last lines of verse for 'Limbo', Coleridge wrote:

> A lurid thought is growthless dull ~~Nega~~Privation,
> But the Hag, Madness, scalds the Fiends of Hell
> With frenzy-dreams, all incompassible

The first line would reappear, but Coleridge must have realized that the personification that followed was uncomfortably close to the monstrous female figures in earlier poems, such as the lines on the 'fiend hag' in 'Ode on the Departing Year':

> Strange-eyed Destruction! who with many a dream
> Of central fires through nether seas-upthundering
> Soothes her fierce solitude.[37]

As he had long ago abandoned such violently willed personifications, a new ending was attempted, beginning, 'A lurid thought is growthless dull Negation [del] Privation.' Coleridge, as we have seen, seriously rejected the notion of Hell as privation, but he was nevertheless willing to toy with it here. He would, of course, have been familiar with the statement in Donne's third Sermon that 'Privation of the presence of God, is Hell.'[38] The choice of Negation or Privation hardly mattered, since the two ideas were in this context the same. However, Hell and Purgatory, conceptually blurred until this point, are now distinguished: 'Yet that is but a Purgatory Curse | Hell knows a fear far worse, | A fear, a future fate. Tis *positive* ~~*Privation*~~ *Negation!*' By the time he wrote these

[37] *CPW* i. 168, ll. 141–3. I refer to the poem by what I believe to be its only correct title.
[38] *The Sermons of John Donne*, ed. George R. Potter and Evelyn M. Simpson (10 vols., Berkeley and Los Angeles: University of California Press, 1962), i. 186. Compare Donne's verse letter, 'To Mr. T. W.': 'And 'tis decreed our hell is but privation | Of him, at least in this earths habitation', *John Donne: The Satires, Epigrams, and Verse Letters*, ed. W. Milgate (Oxford: Clarendon Press, 1967) 61. See George Whalley in *CM* ii. 218, and Kathleen Coburn in *CN* iii. 4073 n. John Beer, *Poems*, 426, notes the echo of the 'dull privations' of Donne's 'Nocturnall upon St Lucies Day'. Indeed, the vastated universe of that poem has much in common with the world of 'Limbo'.

lines Coleridge may have provided an alternative last line on the next Notebook page (ƒ 147), or he may have written it as an afterthought: 'Of aye-unepithetable ~~Priv~~ Negation'. The idea of Negation's being 'unepithetable', not subject to characterization, is a brilliant one, as the epithet is a form of identification through language, and the Negation that Coleridge has in mind cannot be so identified.[39]

Coleridge made at least one other attempt to end 'Limbo' differently, in an entry inscribed in his daughter Sara's album and dated 15 October 1827. Interestingly, this shows a revival of his interest in the material over a year before he corresponded with Alaric Watts about it. Under the heading 'An other Fragment, but in a very different style [from that of "Phantom," which preceded it], from a Dream of Purgatory, alias Limbo',[40] he gives a version of ll. 34–55 that differs little from the Notebook draft, and a 10-line ending that is entirely new. Here we have a return to the female evil of the earlier lines, this time, however, not as a personification but as an actual character. Furthermore, Limbo is given a kind of false escape-hatch that turns out to be worse than its alternative:

> In one sole Outlet yawns the Phantom Wall:
> And thorough this, grim road to worser thrall,
> Oft homeward scouring from a Sick Child's Dream
> Old Mother Brownrigg shoots upon a Scream;
> And turning back her Face with hideous Leer
> Leaves Sentry there INTOLERABLE FEAR![41]

'Mother' Elizabeth Brownrigg was a midwife executed in 1767 (and her skeleton exhibited in the Old Bailey) for torturing her apprentices and murdering at least one of them. She was evidently well remembered in the next century, for Blake drew a Visionary Head of her in 1819.[42] Coleridge had inscribed her name, without comment, in a relatively early Notebook entry that Coburn suggests may have had something to do with a parody of Southey in *The Anti-Jacobin* (*CN* i. 1185 and n.).

[39] Beer points out a related passage in *Aids to Reflection*, 322–3: 'Besides that dissolution of our earthly tabernacle, which we call death, there is another death, not the mere negation of Life, but its positive Opposite.'

[40] Purgatory and Limbo are not alternative words in orthodox theology, as Coleridge certainly knew, which once more demonstrates his indifference to such considerations in this text.

[41] Grateful acknowledgement is made to Mrs Joan Coleridge and the Harry Ransom Humanities Research Center of the University of Texas at Austin for permission to quote from this manuscript, and to Professor J. C. C. Mays for drawing my attention to its present location.

[42] See *The Larger Blake-Varley Sketchbook* (London: Christie, Manson and Woods, 21 July 1989), 28.

Both the original and the parody have thematic elements that may have made Coleridge remember either or both. Southey's poem, 'Inscription IV: For the Apartment in Chepstow-Castle where Henry Marten the Regicide was imprisoned Thirty Years',[43] celebrates the regicide as a martyr whose 'ardent mind | Shaped goodliest plans of happiness on earth, | And peace and liberty. Wild dreams!' This millennial state has only been withheld until 'the latter days, | When CHRIST shall come and all things be fulfill'd.' The parody is entitled 'Inscription | For the Door of the Cell in Newgate Where Mrs. Brownrigg, the 'Prentice-cide, was Confined Previous to her Execution.'[44] It cleverly imitates the rhetorical structures and rhythms of Southey's poem, concluding 'but time shall come, | When France shall reign, and laws be all repealed!' In the 1790s Coleridge's interest would have been caught by the millenarian expectations expressed in one poem and parodied in the other; but at the time of writing the lines quoted above the imagery of imprisonment would have been more pertinent, and especially the *Anti-Jacobin*'s portrayal of Brownrigg in Newgate: 'Often have these cells | Echoed her blasphemies, as with shrill voice | She screamed for fresh Geneva.' The word 'Limbo' retains the meaning of a jail, and those 'Ghosts' who use the sole outlet of escape from Limbo Den will encounter this murderous midwife.

This passage ends with a warning that is rather curious, considering its author:

> A lurid thought is growthless dull Negation:
> Yet that is but a Purgatory Curse.
> SHE knows a fear far worse—
> Flee, lest thou hear its name! Flee, rash Imagination!

The alternative ending concludes with Coleridge—who, perhaps more than any other single figure, had asserted, in the *Biographia Literaria* and elsewhere, the high claims of Imagination—banishing the 'rash' Imagination from the realm that it had itself created. This kind of statement of the inadequacy of the imagination is sometimes encountered in Romantic-apocalyptic literature, as in Mary Shelley's *The Last Man*;[45] and, as we have seen, the Limbo constellation borders on the apocalyptic. To end 'Limbo' with the passage in Sara Coleridge's album was certainly a possibility for the *Poetical Works* of 1834, as Henry Nelson

[43] *Poems* (Bristol and London, 1797 [Dec. 1796]), 59–60.
[44] *The Anti-Jacobin* 20 Nov. 1797), 8.
[45] See my Introduction to the World's Classics edn. of *The Last Man* (Oxford: Oxford University Press, 1994), pp. xv–xvi.

Coleridge, who almost certainly assembled the copy-text, could have inserted the lines from his wife's manuscript. This would, however, have pushed the end of 'Limbo' further toward the apocalyptic-grotesque, making more difficult a transition to the verses that follow. Although we cannot say how the decision was made, the ending published in 1834 makes the junction with the section or poem now known as 'Ne Plus Ultra' more feasible. In making this transition, Coleridge and the reader move from the word-play and phantasmagoria of the earlier parts of the text to a serious contemplation of the nature of evil.

The evidence of the Notebook suggests that 'Ne Plus Ultra' was always part of the Limbo constellation in Coleridge's mind. On top of *f* 147 he wrote one line that, as already discussed, belongs to 'Limbo' but was apparently rejected. This line is written in a distinctly finer hand than that of the earlier-written pages. Continuing in this finer hand, Coleridge then wrote out nineteen lines of poetry and then continued with two lines on *f* 147v. These twenty-one lines comprise the poem published as 'Ne Plus Ultra'. Unlike the preceding parts of the Notebook text, they appear not to be a working draft but a fair copy: only two relatively minor corrections appear. Taking up the idea with which 'Limbo' ends, Coleridge addresses Negation itself.

The title 'Ne Plus Ultra' does not appear in the Notebook and may well have been supplied by Henry Nelson Coleridge rather than the poet. The words derive from a tradition in antiquity that after raising the mountains Abile and Calpe on either side of the Strait of Gibraltar, Hercules inscribed there 'Non Plus Ultra' as a warning to navigators not to venture beyond the known world.[46] The title seems at the same time portentous and irrelevant, much like E. H. Coleridge's 'Coeli Enarrant', Yet there is no alternative to using it. The poem itself, as has been widely recognized, takes as its model not Donne but George Herbert.[47] Litany-like in structure, it comprises a series of interjections without forming a grammatically complete sentence. Yet it ends by linking itself to a much earlier poem of Coleridge's, which considerably affects its meaning.

From the beginning, we can see Coleridge straining to establish meaning by every means at his disposal. 'Sole Positive of Night!' takes its departure from the *'positive Negation!'* of the last line of 'Limbo'.

---

[46] See Manifredi Porena's note to Dante's *Inferno*, xxvi. 107–8. *La Divina Commedia di Dante Alighieri* (3 vols., Bologna: Nicola Zannichelli Editore, 1954–5) i. 241; and H. J. Jackson (ed.), *Samuel Taylor Coleridge* (Oxford: Oxford University Press, 1985), 702.

[47] As Angus Fletcher points out, there is a structural resemblance to Herbert's 'Prayer'; 'Positive Negation', 155.

Now the subject is a personification encompassing that oxymoron but undefinable by any physical attributes. In line 2—'Antipathist of Light!'—the first word is a coinage,[48] not the only one in this poem, and line 3 fuses several allusions into 'Primal Scorpion Rod!' The rod is God's, a frequent threat of chastisement in the Old Testament, while the scorpion may come from I Kings 12: 16: 'My father hath chastised you with whips, but I will chastise you with scorpions.' There is also an association here with Aaron's rod, which becomes a serpent when thrown down at God's command (Exod. 7: 8–12). Furthermore, when in Exod. 9: 17 Aaron stretches out the rod, the dust of the land turns into lice—bringing in associations with the beginning of Coleridge's text. All these allusions point to ultimate divine control over 'The one permitted Opposite of God'. Yet its 'Condensed Blackness' admits of no divine spark within its domain. The Antipathist of Light is a permanent threat to any redemptive vision. Coleridge mused on a similar darkness in the prose work entitled 'Of the Divine Ideas': 'If the ray of mental vision decline but a hair's breadth on this side or on that it is instantly strangled in darkness, or becomes an erring light & its own delusion.'[49] In 'Ne Plus Ultra' the darkness is also presented, like Death in *Paradise Lost*, as an image of power:

> Condensed Blackness, and Abysmal Storm
> Compacted to one Sceptre
> Arms thy grasp enorm,
> The Intercepter!
>
> —black it stood as Night,
> Fierce as ten Furies, terrible as Hell,
> And shook a dreadful dart: what seemed his head
> The likeness of a kingly crown had on.
>
> (ii. 670–3)

As we can see, these eight short lines pack in an astonishing variety of associated meanings. The poem continues in this rich, compacted manner to produce its central allusion—'image' seems too visual a word for this decidedly anti-visual poem—to:

> The dragon foul and fell—
> The unrevealable,
> And hidden one, whose breath
> Gives wind and fuel to the fires of Hell!

---

[48] See James C. McCusick, ' "Living Words": Samuel Taylor Coleridge and the Genesis of the *OED*', *Modern Philology*, 90 (1992), 26.
[49] Ms. in the hand of J. H. Green in the Huntington Library (HM 8195), 45.

The dragon's breath is a parody of the Hebrew *ruah*, the wind of the spirit that produces prophetic inspiration, and of the typical Coleridgean use of breath as associated with creativity, as in the 'heavenly breathings' of 'To William Wordsworth'. The principle of Negation inverts the significance of otherwise positive references. The dragon itself is the great red dragon of Revelation 12, with some residue of the personified Destruction of the 'Ode on the Departing Year', as she lies 'By livid fount, or red volcanic stream' with 'lidless dragon-eyes' (144–5). That this poem has a special connection with the early 'Ode' has been generally recognized, but the nature of that connection remains to be elucidated.

'Ne Plus Ultra' concludes with two references to 'the Lampads Seven' to whom alone 'of all th' Angelic State' the nature of the principle of Negation has been revealed. 'Lampads' is another Coleridgean coinage. Derived from the Greek word for lamp, it refers to the 'seven lamps of fire burning before the throne, which are the seven spirits of God' in Rev. 4: 5. According to the *OED* the word is '*poet. rare*', and the first to use it was S. T. Coleridge, in 1796. That is indeed the date of 'Ode on the Departing Year', and critics have recognized that Coleridge intended to cross-reference 'Ne Plus Ultra' and the 'Ode' by the use of this word. However, both the critics and the *OED* need to be corrected on one point. There were no 'Lampads' in the 'Ode on the Departing Year' as originally published in 1796 or in its subsequent published versions of 1797 and 1803. The word first appears in *Sibylline Leaves* in 1817, as part of a revised passage comprising lines 74–9. As no manuscript of this passage is known to exist, we have no way of telling whether it was written before or after 'Ne Plus Ultra'. In other words, it is just as possible that Coleridge wrote the 'Lampads' passage of the 'Ode' to connect with 'Ne Plus Ultra' as vice versa. This brings the two poems into even closer connection. In both, the Lampads introduce a reassuring note to what would otherwise be an extremely pessimistic context. In the 'Ode' that context is political and apocalyptic: the relation of England to the rest of the world is such that apocalyptic destruction is imminent.[50] When in the 1817 version the Lampads give 'permissive signal' to the 'fervent Spirit' before he begins his denunciatory speech, itself much toned-down, an element of theodicy is introduced that at least partially reassures the reader (and perhaps the author as well). However seemingly anarchic the world may be, there is, though mysterious to us, divine governance. In 'Ne Plus Ultra' the

---

[50] See my 'Apocalypse and Millennium in the Poetry of Coleridge', *TWC* 23 (1992), 24–34.

context is theological. If the true nature of the 'Antipathist of Light' has been revealed to the Lampads Seven, divine control is asserted. The poem is not dualistic, as some believe, about the nature of God. 'The Dragon foul and fell' is irredeemable, as in Revelation; but, also as in Revelation, its power is divinely contained.

The question remains: what did the Lampads mean to Coleridge, who introduced them into the English language? A gloss may be provided in part by a passage in the tenth of the *Philosophical Lectures*, where the seven spirits of God are paralleled with the Sephiroth of the Kabala:

> The Deity considered in himself and in his own essential nature they [the Kabalists] represented as three in one; but the Deity as manifested as expanding <*in at*> least <*seven*> ways, they represented as the seven spirits or the seven Sephiroth. The last, which was to be the Messiah or the Shekinah, was to be the second person of the triad, and to be in the Shekinah a concentration of all the seven spirits of the manifestation, a doctrine which must have been very early indeed in the Church, because we find a clear reference to it in the Apocalypse.[51]

Coleridge well knew that there were ten Sephiroth, but he follows a Christian tradition in dividing them into the mystical numbers of three and seven.[52] The culminating reference to Revelation makes clear Coleridge's idea of the seven spirits as not merely lamps or even angels but, taken as a whole, as a manifestation of the Messiah. As he put it in a note on *The Origin of Arianism Disclosed* by John Whitaker (1810): 'The *seven spirits* = 10 *Sephiroth*, constituting together the *Adam Kadmon*, the second Adam of St. Paul, the incarnate one in the Messiah.'[53] Coleridge's notion is similar to Blake's idea of the Seven Eyes of God, a sequence of manifestations of divinity, of which the seventh is Jesus. The discussion of the seven spirits in *Philosophical Lectures* underscores for us the strongly positive nature of the ending of 'Ne Plus Ultra' with its reiterated Lampads.

At the bottom of *f*146v—that is, after the last line of 'Limbo' as it is usually published—Coleridge wrote: 'A Specimen of the Sublime dashed to pieces by cutting too close with her fiery Four in Hand round the corner of Nonsense—' This ironic comment on the text is also a part of it, as much so as T. S. Eliot's 'That was a way of putting it—not

[51] *Philosophical Lectures*, 299.

[52] See Fulford, *Coleridge's Figurative Language*, 133; and 'Apocalyptic and Reactionary: Coleridge as Hermenutist?', *Modern Language Review*, 87 (1992), 22–5.

[53] *Complete Works of Samuel Taylor Coleridge*, ed. W. G. T. Shedd (7 vols., New York, 1884) v. 453. *Cf. CN* iv. 4870: 'But the Spirit = 7 Spirits of God rest in plenitude on the Messiah.'

very satisfactory' in 'East Coker'.[54] Like Eliot, Coleridge had wrestled
with words and meanings, aware of the limitations of language. 'The
Sublime' becomes one of the personifications of 'Limbo', a female
charioteer who, like the 'Ghosts', endures torment—in her case *sparag-
mos*, being torn to pieces by the destructive power of nonsense. Yet as
we have seen, 'nonsense' is endemic to 'Limbo'. The problem, if any,
lies not so much in cutting too close to the corner as in not going far
enough. As Harold Bloom remarks, this is 'not a Counter-Sublime but
a negative Sublime'.[55] In the Limbo constellation, Coleridge created
out of his personal sense of devastation a work which explores various
phases of being, first ironically, then in a series of surreal images, and
last in nine exclamations probing the nature of evil. Its final vision,
though dark, is one of reconciliation, and may be aptly paralleled with
its author's statement at the beginning of the end of the *Biographia
Literaria* about 'the unity of the one power by relative opposites':

It is Eternity revealing itself in the Phenomena of time: and the perception and
acknowledgment of the proportionality and appropriateness of the Present to
the Past, prove to the afflicted Soul, that it has not yet been deprived of the
sight of God, that it can still recognize the effective presence of a Father,
though through a darkened glass and a turbid atmosphere, though of a Father
that is chastising it.[56]

54 *Collected Poems 1909–62* (London: Faber & Faber, 1963), 198.
55 Harold Bloom, Introduction to his Modern Critical Views anthology, *Samuel Taylor
Coleridge* (New York: Chelsea House, 1986), 15.
56 *Biographia Literaria*, ii. 234.

The study of Samuel Taylor Coleridge

3 SELF

1816 began a new epoch in Coleridge's life when he came to live with James and Anne Gillman at Highgate. James Gillman, a surgeon, did his best to control Coleridge's opium habit; and both James and Anne provided the poet with the personal warmth and domestic stability that he so desperately needed. At just about this time, Coleridge's professional status as a man of letters was reinforced by a series of publications. In 1816, two of his most famous poems saw print for the first time when John Murray published the volume comprising 'Christabel', 'Kubla Khan', and 'The Pains of Sleep'. Later that year appeared *The Statesman's Manual*, a new prose work, to be followed by another, *A Lay Sermon*, the following year. In 1817 *Sibylline Leaves*, in the press since 1815, was published, as was the *Biographia Literaria*. And although, unlike Coleridge's stage success *Remorse*, the play *Zapolya* was not performed, it too was published in 1817. The sum total of these events, personal and public, re-established Coleridge's sense of himself and gave him the confidence to contemplate ambitious projects once more. As Mary Lynn Johnson astutely remarks of a copy of *Sibylline Leaves* annotated by Coleridge,

It provides a vignette of Coleridge in his early forties, not in his character as addict, lecturer, and sage of Highgate, but as an active practising poet, struggling to shape fresh ideas and images, pausing to reflect on the processes of composition and revision, and thrashing out practical problems with his publishers, reviewers, and other writers.[1]

At first, however, Coleridge's energies were not directed to writing lyric poetry. In 1818 he gave his fourteen lectures on European literature for the London Philosophical Society, republished *The Friend* in three volumes, and contributed his 'Treatise on Method' to the *Encylopaedia Metropolitana*. During the winter of 1818–19 he delivered his philosophical lectures and his lectures on Shakespeare. It was probably not until 1823 that the urge to write lyric poetry presented itself in a form not to be denied, as recorded by Coleridge in a Notebook entry that he carefully dated '10 September 1823. Wednesday Morning. 10 o'clock'

---

[1] 'How Rare Is a "Unique Annotated Copy" of Coleridge's *Sibylline Leaves*?' *Bulletin of the New York Public Library*, 452.

(*CN* iv. 4994). Two months later, Coleridge and the Gillmans moved to No. 3, The Grove, in Highgate; and Coleridge took the attic for his bed-and-book-room. The poet took delight in this room, praising its 'view over Southampton Farm, Kenn Wood, & Hampstead not surpassed within a hundred miles of London',[2] and it was here that the poetry of his last decade was written.

One of the central subjects of that poetry is Coleridge's self. Representation of the self had always been important to Coleridge, as in poems such as 'The Eolian Harp', 'Frost At Midnight', 'This Lime-Tree Bower My Prison', and 'France: An Ode'. In these and other poems of his early maturity, he plays numerous roles—lover and quasi-mystic, father musing on his own childhood, disabled poet, former revolutionary sympathizer. One might expect Coleridge's later poetry to manifest deeper probings of the self, considering the almost obsessive capacity for self-analysis demonstrated in his Notebooks and the fact that, whether or not he introduced 'psychological' to the English language, he did much to acclimatize it there.[3] However, the purpose of self-representation in the later poetry is dramatic rather than analytic. Coleridge typically casts himself in a single role, though different aspects of it may be emphasized. He is the wise old man who pays for his wisdom with lack of human fulfilment, reaching out to others for friendship, having renounced the possibility of love. Obviously, this persona is intimately related to Coleridge's actual life situation, yet it is important to emphasize that it *is* a persona; certain aspects of his existence have been screened out and others emphasized in order to make the poetry possible. This can be seen in five poems of the 1820s: 'Youth and Age', in which he makes an elegiac lyric out of his own infirmity; 'Work without Hope', where a moment of despair is artistically crystallized; 'Lines Suggested by the Last Words of Berengarius', in which the poet reflects about himself in the thin guise of an eleventh-century

[2] Letter to John Anster dated 18 Feb. 1824, *CL* v. 335. As this room is so identified with Coleridge's Highgate years, it is worth pointing out that the view described by Coleridge is *not* that memorably recreated by Thomas Carlyle looking over 'the illimitable limitary ocean of London, with its domes and steeples definite in the sun', in *The Life of John Sterling* (London, 1897), 54. As John Beer has pointed out to me, Carlyle must have imagined the view from Coleridge's previous residence, Moreton House, as he met Coleridge only in 1824, after the move to The Grove. A more reliable description is provided in *The Autobiography of Leigh Hunt*, ed. J. E. Morpurgo (London, 1948), 288.

[3] See *Lectures 1808–19*, where Coleridge is recorded as saying that he should be inclined 'to pursue a psychological, rather than a historical, mode of reasoning' about Shakespeare's dramas (ii. 236). R. A. Foakes notes that the *OED* gives an example of a published use of 'psychological' in 1812, earlier than Coleridge's first published use; but as this lecture was delivered on 23 Nov. 1811, it would of course have priority.

theologian; 'The Improvisatore', a self-dramatization of the poet as one whose art must compensate for unattainable love; and 'The Garden of Boccaccio', a reverie combining the present experience of a work of art with memories of Italy. All five involve the interplay of the past and the present and of Coleridge's own past and present as they would have been known to his readers through his poetry, as part of a process of self-definition.

'Youth And Age'

'Youth and Age' is a poem that was much admired in Coleridge's lifetime and later in the nineteenth century. A favourite of the poet's—he even referred to it as an 'ode' (see below), it was described by Leigh Hunt as 'one of the most perfect poems, for style, feeling, and everything, that were ever written'; and it was one of only two poems by Coleridge included in the original *Golden Treasury*.[4] One has the sense, however, that today the poem's admirers are as few as they are fit, perhaps because it is so seldom reprinted outside of Coleridge's complete poetical works. Yet the poem combines a dazzling technical mastery with a self-representation prefiguring Yeats's in poems such as 'Sailing to Byzantium', with its tragic sense of an inner being trapped in a deteriorating body.

Coleridge was thinking in terms of the basic contrast of 'Youth and Age' as early as as 1819–20 (see *CN* iv. 4632, though here the idea could equally be related to the already-published 'Time, Real and Imaginary'). The actual writing of the poem (in NB 3½, BL Add. MS 47499) seems to have begun in September 1823, with a beautiful prose reminiscence of the Quantock Hills, and an air that whizzed by:

at earliest Dawn, just between the Nightingale I had stopt to hear in the copse at the foot of Quantock, and the <first> Sky-Lark that was a Song-Fountain, dashing up and sparkling to the Ear's Eye, in full Column, or ornamental Shaft of Sound in the order of Gothic Extravagance, out of Sight, over the Cornfields on the Descent of the Mountain on the other side out of sight, tho' twice I beheld its *mute* shoot downward in the sunshine like a falling Star of melted Silver—

(*CN* iv. 4994)

[4] *Imagination and Fancy* (New York, 1845 [1844]), 213; *The Golden Treasury*, ed. Francis Turner Palgrave (Cambridge and London: Macmillan, 1861), 294–5.

There follows, under the heading *Aria Spontanea*, a version of what became lines 18 ff. of 'Youth and Age'. After an intervening entry,[5] Coleridge wrote a draft or version of the first part of the poem, then went on into a version of the second part, and continued on with a few lines of a third part beginning 'Dew-drops are the Gems of Morning' (*CN* iv. 4996). He later made two fair copies, differing in some details from each other, and sent one, on paper watermarked 1826, to Alaric Watts, editor of *The Literary Souvenir*.[6] It appeared in that annual in the autumn of 1827 as well as in two other publications with which Watts was associated, the *Standard* (20 October 1827) and *The St. James Chronicle* (18–20 October 1827); and it also was published in William Pickering's annual *The Bijou* before appearing in the *Poetical Works* of 1828.[7] It was thus one of the most widely disseminated of Coleridge's later poems.

One of the most striking features of 'Youth and Age' is its musicality. In 1832 Coleridge divided poetry into two classes, the one corresponding to poetry, the other to music. 'If I belong to any class of poets it is most preeminently the latter,' he said.[8] It is this aspect of the poem that is hardest to discuss subtly, without seeming grossly mechanical. As originally published, 'Youth and Age' comprises four units, the first and third of which are each dithyrambic quatrains followed by a short unrhymed exclamatory line, the second and fourth longer lyrical reflections in iambic tetrameter couplets. The short sections display a great deal of variety. In the first, iambic and trochaic lines alternate; feminine rhymes in lines 1 and 3 add to the lilting quality, and the fifth line consists of two spondaic feet. The rhyming couplets of section 2 are basically iambic, but when section 3 begins it surprises the ear by first beginning with a trochee, leading one to expect a repetition of the pattern, only to follow with four iambs (as in line one, the inital line has five feet, and the following three have four). Once more there are feminine rhymes, this time compounded ('flower-like'/'shower-like') and again the fifth line of the section is made up of two spondees. The two five-line sections thus display a mixture of predictable order and unpredictable variety that Coleridge knew would interest the ear. The two longer sections, in contrast, are comparatively regular in sound-pattern but

[5] Coburn, however, cautions against taking the dated entry 4993 as necessarily referring to the composition of the poetry in 4994.

[6] Manuscripts in the PML and in the John Rylands Library. I am grateful to Professor J. C. C. Mays for this information.

[7] See *CL* vi. 710–11 n. According to Coleridge, the *Bijou* publication was without his knowledge or consent.

[8] *Table Talk* i. 270–3 (31 Mar. 1832).

present a rapid succession of vivid images. This combination of qualities is not merely a bravura technical performance. It is a moving self-representation, producing a deep pathos in its contrast of past and present selves.

Portraits of the later Coleridge as a frail-looking, prematurely aged man with completely white hair bear witness to the picture he gives of himself in 'Youth and Age'. The poet laments the change in 'this breathing house not built with hands'—a memorable line achieved after several changes: the Notebook draft first read 'This poor house'; that was changed to 'This house of Life', which then became 'This house of clay'. The final reading, that of the three *Poetical Works*, first appeared in *The Literary Souvenir*. Embedded here is a reference to 2 Cor. 5: 1: 'For know that if our earthly house of this tabernacle were dissolved, we have a building of God, an house not made with hands, eternal in the heavens.'[9] But while in his earthly house, Coleridge bitterly feels it is 'This body, that does me grievous wrong'. In contrast Coleridge thinks of his past self, the Coleridge who as a young man spent nine days walking and climbing alone, traversing the sandy beach at St. Bees, climbing England's highest peak, Scafell, and descending by a series of drops from ledge to ledge.[10]

> O'er aery cliffs and glittering sands,
> How lightly then it flashed along:—.

The statement, originally 'O'er hill and dale and glittering sands',[11] has once more been made less conventional and more vivid.

Next the past self is troped to

> those trim skiffs, unknown of yore,
> On winding lakes and rivers wide,
> That ask no aid of sail or oar,
> That fear no spite of wind or tide!

Although the word 'skiff' is not usually used for a power-driven vessel,[12] the only kind that would need no help of sail or oar would be a steamboat, such as those that Coleridge saw during his seaside holidays at Ramsgate. Coleridge originally wrote 'boats', and this is the word that

---

[9] A passage also alluded to in *Aids to Reflection*, 15: 'none then, not one of human kind, so poor and destitute, but there is provided for him, even in his present state, *a house not built with hands*.'

[10] Letters to Sara Hutchinson, 1–5 Aug. 1802 and 6 Aug. 1802 (*CL* i. 834–45). See also *CN* i. 1205–28.

[11] So in the Notebook, in the manuscript called 'MS 1' by E. H. Coleridge (*CPW* i. 439 n.), and *The Bijou*.

[12] Cf. the 'skiff-boat' that is rowed in *The Rime of the Ancient Mariner* (*CPW* i. 206, l. 523).

appeared in 'MS 1' and in *The Bijou*. However nautically imprecise it may be, 'skiffs' has more of a sense of darting, forward motion. In these lines we can see how Coleridge created a series of antitheses that he made even sharper in the process of revision. Even abstractions could be honed finer. 'The joys, that came down showerlike' were originally 'Beauty, Truth, and Liberty'; these became 'Friendship, Love, and Liberty'[13]—more personal qualities that also represent more accurately the joys that the young Coleridge had actually celebrated in writing of the French Revolution and of Pantisocracy.

Ironically, the roles of disguise and true appearance become reversed as the speaker is imagined as desperately striving to evade the truth about the loss of his youth:

> It cannot be that thou art gone!
> Thy vesper-bell hath not yet toll'd:—
> And thou wert aye a masker bold!
> What strange disguise hast now put on,
> To make believe, that thou art gone?

Coleridge now puts a distance between himself as poet and himself as speaker and subject. Youth's 'disguise' is of course not Age, no matter how many other masks Youth may have worn. Yet the speaker is shocked by his own image. Personal observation and traditional *topos* now combine:

> I see these locks in silvery slips,
> This drooping gait, this altered size . . .

The silvery hair is that of the traditional *senex*-figure, as in the 'Sonet' that concludes George Peele's *Polyhymnia*; and it indeed seems likely that Coleridge was indeed thinking of that well-known poem:

> His golden lockes, Time hath to Silver turn'd,
>   O Time too swift, o Swiftnesse never ceasing:
> His youth gainst time and Age have ever spurn'd
> But spurn'd in vain, Youth waineth by increasing.
>   Beauty, Strength, Youth, are flowers, but fading seen,
>   Dutie, Faith, Love, are roots, and ever green.[14]

---

[13] Once more, the earlier reading is that of the Notebook, 'MS 1', and *The Bijou*, but not of *The Literary Souvenir*. Alaric Watts seems to have received a sort of poetic justice in getting the manuscript with the readings that in most cases Coleridge wanted to preserve. An exception is l. 23, where 'Ah woful Ere' is the reading of all published versions except *The Literary Souvenir*, which has 'Ah, mournful Ere'.

[14] David H. Horne, *The Life and Minor Works of George Peele* (New Haven; Yale University Press, 1952), 244. As Horne notes, the attribution of the 'Sonnet' to Peele has been questioned.

In its originally published forms, the poem then reached a fine closure with the speaker's decision to continue to deceive himself:

> Life is but thought: so think I will
> That youth and I are house-mates still.

However, in the 'deathbed edition' of 1834 a third stanza is introduced, incorporating material that had already been published in a separate poem in 1832. Whether this added stanza is accepted by the reader as part of 'Youth and Age' will, of course, depend at least in part on the reader's view of the *Poetical Works* of 1834. It can at least be said that Coleridge had previously considered the possibility of a third stanza and had rejected it, giving a highly convincing reason.

'Youth and Age' and 'An Old Man's Sigh'

In the manuscript known as 'The Berg Notebook' (Berg Collection, NYPL), Coleridge wrote ten lines under the heading 'Fragment of the intended third Stanza to Youth and Age':

> III
> Dewdrops are the *Gems* of Morning
> But the *Tears* of mournful Eve:
> Where no Hope is, Life's a warning
> That only serves to make us grieve,
>   With long leave taking!
>   In our Old Age!
> With long leave taking, like a Guest
> That may not rudely be dismiss'd
> Yet hath outstay'd—xx Caetera desunt[15]

The first four lines, which had appeared in the Notebook draft of September 1823 (*CN* iv. 4996), are indeed beautiful, with their transformation of gems to tears. Their rhythm is, of course, that of the opening stanzas of the two preceding parts, and they take up the theme of hope introduced at the beginning of the poem. The subsequent image of the guest who has outstayed his welcome is a moving expression of Coleridge's awareness of being a man who lived in other people's houses. Nevertheless, the poet decided not to include the 'intended third stanza'. His reason for doing has to do with his concern for the

---

[15] This is evidently the passage transcribed (with minor variations) from an otherwise unidentified 'notebook' by Warren E. Gibbs, 'S. T. Coleridge's "The Knight's Tomb" and "Youth and Age" ', *Modern Language Review*, 28 (1933), 84–5.

relation of the part to the whole, a concern we have already discussed with respect to 'Love, Hope, and Patience in Education'.

But the former forms a whole without it: and I must have made a cheerless conclusion or a religious one too elevated for the character of the ode. But there is for *my* ear a sweetness in the movement of the first four lines, that makes them well worth writing down.[16]

Indeed, they were so well worth writing down that Coleridge did so in various places on various occasions, sometimes with additions and variations, as in a manuscript in the Cornell Wordsworth Collection dated 18 May 1829:

Youth and Age

Dew-drops are the Gems of Morning,
But the Tears of mournful Eve:
Where no Hope is, Life's a Warning
That only serves to make us grieve,
As we creep feebly down life's slope,
Yet, courteous dame, accept this truth,
Hope leaves us not, but we leave hope,
And quench the inward light of youth.[17]

Here we can see Coleridge searching for some use to make of the fine lines he had not chosen to include as part of a third stanza of 'Youth and Age', which appeared in two-stanza form in the *Poetical Works* of 1828 and that of 1829. Only the first four of these lines were ever printed by Coleridge, and they first appeared not as part of 'Youth and Age' but in a new context, as part of 'an English Sonnet'.

In *Blackwood's* for June 1832, Coleridge published 'An Old Man's Sigh: A Sonnet', dated 18 May 1832 and preceded by a surprisingly bad-tempered piece of prose. In this single long paragraph headed 'What Is an English Sonnet?' Coleridge, described his new poem as 'the following-Out-Slough, or hypertrophic Stanza, of a certain poem called "Youth and Age" '; and continuing what might be described as the downside of a typical Coleridgean organic metaphor, declared that 'having, by a judicial ligature of the Verse-maker's own tying, detached itself, and dropt off from the poem aforesaid, [it] assumes the name and

[16] The entry is undated; on the next Notebook page is the poem 'An Elegiac Plusquam to my Tin Shaving pot', dated Jany. 1st, 1832. Of course the pages need not necessarily have been filled in chronological order, and 'Cetaera desunt' [the others are not there] suggests that additional lines existed somewhere.

[17] Coleridge wrote these same lines, with very minor variations, in a lady's album in Brussels in 1828, and they were printed by Colley Grattan in his *Beaten Paths; And Those Who Trod Them* (2 vols., London: Chapman & Hall, 1862), i. 139.

rank of an integral Animal'.[18] The poem that follows begins with lines that are indeed closely associated, rhythmically and thematically, with 'Youth and Age', but then goes into territory of its own:

> Dew-drops are the gems of morning,
> But the tears of mournful eve!
> Where no hope is, life's a warning
> That only serves to make us grieve
> When we are old:
> In our old age
> Whose bruised wings quarrel with the bars of the still narrowing cage.
> That only serves to make us grieve
> With oft and tedious taking leave,
> Like some poor nigh-related guest,
> That may not rudely be dismist;
> Yet hath outstay'd his welcome while,
> And tells the jest without the smile.
> O might life cease! and Selfless Mind
> Whose total Being is Act, remain behind.

The most remarkable aspects of this fifteen-line (counting the half-length lines 5 and 6) 'sonnet' are the interpolated seventh line and the new ending. Line 7 brilliantly captures the theme of self-entrapment that is conveyed through different imagery in the part of 'Work without Hope' that Coleridge did not publish (see below), as well as anticipating Gerard Manley Hopkins's 'dare-gale skylark in a cage'; and yet the image is oddly unrelated to anything else in this poem. The two final lines evidently stem from Coleridge's desire to refute the materialist, corpuscular theory of life. 'This theory,' wrote Seth B. Watson in his preface to Coleridge's posthumously published *Theory of Life*, 'Mr. Coleridge combats. The supposed atoms, he says, are mere abstractions of the mind; and Life is not a thing, the result of atomic arrangement or action, but is itself an act, or process.'[19] The last two lines, indeed, express such an idea in such a way as to bear out Coleridge's expressed disinclination for a conclusion 'Too elevated for the character of the ode'; although 'hollow' might be a better word than 'elevated'. Furthermore,

---

[18] *Blackwood's Edinburgh Magazine*, 31 (1832), 956. A version sent in a letter to J. H. Green on 18 May 1832 (PML MA 1856) was written out as prose but when arranged as verse as in *CL* vi. 910 comes to 13 lines, lacking lines 5 and 6 of the poem as published in *Blackwood's*. There may have been a scribal omission, as the letter makes it clear that Coleridge thinks he is sending a 14-line poem. For other manuscript versions see J. C. C. Mays's edition of the *Poetical Works*.

[19] *Hints Towards the Formation of a More Comprehensive Theory of Life* (London, 1848), 11. This connection was first suggested in *JDC* 641.

the persona that we encounter in 'An Old Man's Sigh' is not the one that Coleridge presents to his readers in 'Youth and Age' and his other late poems. In these he shows himself, however tinged with pathos or even despair, as a dignified figure, stoically bearing the vicissitudes of physical infirmity, the lack of fulfilment in love, and consequent periods of despair. The embittered old man who speaks in 'An Old Man's Sigh' is foreign to the characteristic self-representation of Coleridge's later poetry.

Coleridge evidently recognized these problems, for neither line 7 nor the last two lines appeared again in his lifetime. Indeed, 'An Old Man's Sigh' is absent from the *Poetical Works* of 1834. However, 'Youth and Age' appeared there with the third stanza that in his Notebook entry the poet had given good reason not to include. The stanza essentially comprises the sonnet divested of its fifth, thirteenth, and fourteenth lines. As this material existed in manuscript before the publication of 'An Old Man's Sigh', but was not used in the *Poetical Works* of 1828 or 1829, it is hard to escape the conclusion that Henry Nelson Coleridge's influence was at work here. Those who insist upon the principle that the last lifetime edition must always determine the texts we use may not wish to depart from it here, despite the special circumstances of the 'deathbed edition'.[20] Nevertheless, despite the strength of individual parts, the third stanza seems an anticlimax coming after a the strong closure of lines 37–8, while the two-strophe 'Youth and Age' is complete in itself and one of the great achievements of Coleridge's later poetry.

'Work without Hope'

February 1825 was an unusually warm month in Britain. The *Annual Register* for 1825 reported that the temperature was as high as 54 degrees. *The Times* reported on February 2 (page 2) that it was difficult for confectioners to obtain ice, and on February 3 (page 3):

Last week the weather was so mild in Annandale, that the bees were beginning to buzz about as in May or June. The fields are covered with a verdure like that of spring, and the wheat braird, though late is thriving well.

[20] It is only fair to record that a critic as perceptive as Max Schulz prefers the 1834 version on poetic grounds, remarking: 'Thus revised, the final structure of "Youth and Age", while dialectically opposing the present to the past, interweaves a dense complex of motifs: youth–age, freedom–confinement, joy–sorrow, immutability–mutability, nature–man, union–isolation, beloved–friendless.' *The Poetic Voices of Coleridge* (Detroit, 1963), 143–4. However, most of these antitheses are present in the two-stanza version and are in fact the basis upon which the poem is structured.

In this midwinter spring, on February 21 as he recorded in the MS
known as 'The Clasped Vellum Notebook' (Berg Collection, NYPL),
Coleridge wrote what was to become one of his best-known later
poems, beginning with a depiction of nature awakening to a life of work
from which the poet feels cut off:

> All Nature seems at work. Slugs leave their lair—
> The bees are stirring—birds are on the wing—

The evocation of the scaled-down nature of a Highgate garden, abetted
by the liquids' slowing of 'Slugs leave their lair'[21] is especially fine.
There follows a personification that, as in a number of the later poems,
revives a convention of the eighteenth century with a trope one can
easily imagine William Blake humanizing, as in one of his illustrations
to the poems of Gray.

> And Winter slumbering in the open air,
> Wears on his smiling face a dream of Spring!

The basic contrast becomes that presented in stanza 2 of Wordsworth's
'Ode: Intimations of Immortality'.

> Now, while the birds thus sing a joyous song,
>   And while the young lambs bound
>   As to the tabor's sound,
> To me alone there came a thought of grief:[22]

Yet the auspicious details of Coleridge's first four lines do not precede a
regeneration of the poet as they do in Wordsworth's 'Ode', where 'A
timely utterance gave that thought relief, | And I again am strong'
(23–4). Instead, the speaker sees himself as permanently sundered
from the ongoing activity of the natural world:

> And I the while, the sole unbusy thing,
> Nor honey make, nor pair, nor build, nor sing.

In contrasting his inert self with the bees making honey, Coleridge, as
his daughter Sara noted in her copy of the *Poetical Works* of 1834, drew
on George Herbert's 'Employment': 'All things are busie; only I |
Neither bring honey with the bees'[23]; and Ernest Hartley Coleridge
suggested another parallel in the last stanza of Herbert's 'Praise' (1):

[21] Coleridge originally wrote 'Snails' but substituted 'Slugs'. The word was misprinted
'Stags' in the *Poetical Works* of 1828 and of 1829, but was given correctly in that of 1834.

[22] *Poems in Two Volumes*, ed. Jared Curtis (Princeton, NJ; Princeton University Press,
1983), 271–2.

[23] *The Works of George Herbert*, ed. F. E. Hutchinson (Oxford: Clarendon Press, 1945
[1941]), 57. See Derrick Woolf, 'Sara Coleridge's Marginalia', *The Coleridge Bulletin*, N.S. no.
2 (Autumn 1993), 11. Coleridge was annotating Herbert in June 1824, as George Whalley
points out in *CM* ii. 1033, 1035.

> O raise me then! Poore bees that work all day,
>   Sting my delay,
> Who have a work as well as they,
>   And much, much more.[24]

Wordsworth had similarly set himself off in 'Resolution and Independence' from 'the sklylark warbling in the sky' and 'the playful hare' to ask:

> But how can he expect that others should
> Build for him, sow for him, and at his call
> Love him, who for himself will take no heed at all?[25]

Yet Herbert *expects* to be raised, and Wordsworth recovers his powers after encountering the Leech Gatherer. Coleridge's poem presents no such solutions, not even when in line 5 'the sole unbusy thing' seems almost to prompt a reply from Matt 6: 26: 'Behold the fowls of the air: for they sow not, neither do they reap, nor gather into barns; yet your heavenly Father feedeth them.' Instead, the word 'Thing' assigns the poet the status of a lifeless object, and the poem turns to the landscape of his past achievements only to create another negative contrast.

> Yet well I ken the banks where amaranths blow,
> Have traced the fount where streams of nectars flow.

Next to 'Amaranths' in his Notebook text, Coleridge placed a mark with the the note: '*Literally* rendered is Flower Fadeless, or never-fading—from the Greek—a *not* and marainô, to wither.' Coleridge would, of course, have been familiar with the importance Milton assigns the amaranth in the unfallen Paradise and in Heaven:

> Immortal amarant, a flower which once
> In Paradise, fast by the Tree of Life,
> Began to bloom; but soon for Man's offence
> To Heaven removed, where first it grew, there grows,
> And flowers aloft, shading the Fount of Life,
> And where the River of Bliss through midst of Heaven
> Rolls o'er Elysian flowers her amber stream!
>   (*Paradise Lost* iii. 353–9)

This immortal flower has an important place in Coleridge's imaginative world, and his reference to it draws upon associations established in earlier poems. In a manuscript version of 'To a Young Lady, with a poem on the French Revolution' (1794), the poet turns from the ferocious energies of Revolutionary France to say, 'With wearied thought I

---

[24] *CPW* i. 447 n.; *The Works of George Herbert*, 61.
[25] *Poems in Two Volumes*, 123–4.

seek the amaranth shade'.[26] Perhaps because he wished to avoid ming-
ling the amaranth of friendship with the myrtle of marriage that appears in the next line, Coleridge eliminated the former. Here he may
have been following a distinction made by Charlotte Smith, one that
would later become prominent in 'The Improvisatore': 'For you, fair
Friendship's amaranth shall blow, | And Love's own thornless roses
bind your head!'[27] Thomas Chatterton, who for Coleridge as for many
of his contemporaries, was an example of the poet as hero and martyr, is
troped as 'An Amaranth, which earth scarce seem'd to own' in 'On
Observing a Blossom on the First of February 1796' (*CPW* i. 148). This
never-dying flower is also prominent in 'Religious Musings', in a passage that Coleridge singled out for reprinting in the *Biographia
Literaria* as indicative of the millennialism of his youthful self:

> The massy gates of Paradise are thrown
> Wide open, and forth comes in fragments wild
> Sweet echoes of unearthly melodies,
> And odours snatched from beds of Amaranth.[28]

When Coleridge writes, 'Yet well I ken the banks where amaranths
blow' in 'Work without Hope', he stirs associations of poems in which
the flower signified friendship, poetic immortality, and the hope of a
historical millennium. It is long since that word appeared in his poetry,
and he now assigns it to others:

> Bloom, O ye amaranths, bloom for whom ye may,
> For me ye bloom not!

The initial stress in line 5, seeming at first to convey a sense of resolution, only makes the poet's renunciation more poignant.

The poet's 'wreathless brow' in line 11 again brings up a stream of
references, both to Coleridge himself and to Wordsworth, similar to
that discussed in Chapter 1. Wordsworth could declare 'My head hath
its coronal' in the 'Intimations' Ode[29]; but Coleridge has renounced the
wreath as he has the amaranth, even coining the word 'wreathless' for
the purpose.[30] He now wanders in a landscape that resembles those of
the *Paradise Lost* passage quoted above and (as many readers have

---

[26] *CPW* i. 65 n. This ms. of the poem is part of Coleridge's letter to Robert Southey, 21 Oct.
1794.

[27] Sonnet 20, *Elegiac Sonnets*, 7th edn. (London, 1795), 20.

[28] *CPW* i. 122, ll. 346–9. The wording differs slightly in *BL*. Coburn (*CN* iv. 5192 n) notes
Martin Luther's use of this flower as an image of renewal in *Colloquia Mensalia* (1652).

[29] *Poems in Two Volumes*, 272.

[30] See James C. McCusick, ' "Living Words": Samuel Taylor Coleridge and the Genesis of
the *OED*', *Modern Philology*, 90 (1992), 45.

noticed) one of his own his greatest creations—'Kubla Khan'. 'The founts where streams of nectar flow' combines reminiscences of the 'mighty fountain' of the earlier poem with the 'honey-dew' of its penultimate line; but the poet here is not the mantic figure who has drunk the milk of Paradise, but someone whose lips are 'unbrightened'— another Coleridgean coinage,[31] substituting for 'unmoist' in the manuscript. His very motion—'I stroll'—suggests abandonment to lassitude. This is the Coleridge to whose 'alderman-after dinner pace' John Keats referred after their memorable meeting in a lane near Kenwood in 1819.[32] Then, in the concluding couplet, Coleridge returns to the theme of the loss of Hope, which, as we have seen, is so important in the later poetry:

> Work without Hope draws nectar in a sieve,
> And Hope without an object cannot live.[33]

The consequences of the failure of hope continued to preoccupy him. 'Hope . . . above all things,' he said in *A Lay Sermon* (1817), 'distinguishes the free man from the slave.'[34] Later, in *On the Constitution of the Church and State* (1830), he wrote: 'Our Maker has distinguished man from the brute that perishes, by making hope first an instinct of his nature; and secondly, an indispensable condition of his moral and intellectual progression'; he then went on, significantly, to quote Wordsworth:

> For every gift of noble origin
> Is breathed upon by Hope's perpetual breath.[35]

Unable to make the Wordsworthian recuperation, the Hope-less poet is a slave, a 'Thing'. Yet, paradoxically, he compensates. Just as Herbert, though he made no honey, began his 'Praise': 'To write a verse or two is all the praise, | That I can raise,'[36] Coleridge makes one of his best late

---

[31] 'Living Words', 43.

[32] Letter to George and Georgiana Keats, 14 Feb.–3 May 1819. *Letters of John Keats*, ed. Hyder Edward Rollins, (Cambridge, Mass.: Harvard University Press, 1958), ii. 88. Significantly, one of the subjects Coleridge spoke of was 'single and double touch' (ii. 89); see n. 61 below.

[33] These lines, Kathleen Coburn has shown, draw upon the text and engraving in Francis Quarles's *Emblems, Divine, and Moral* (1736), Book I, no. xii. 'Reflections in a Coleridge Mirror: Some Images in His Poems', *From Sensibility to Romanticism*, ed. Frederick Hilles and Harold Bloom (New York; Oxford University Press, 1965), 425–7.

[34] *Lay Sermons*, 227.

[35] *On the Constitution of the Church and State*, 73. The Wordsworth quotation comprises lines 10–11 of the 20th of the Sonnets Dedicated to Independence and Liberty, headed 'October 1803' and beginning 'These times strike moneyed worldlings with dismay', *Poems in Two Volumes*, 169.   [36] *The Poems of George Herbert*, 61.

poems out of his inability to recapture the state of self of his earlier
poetry, continuing, in so doing, a theme that he had himself begun in
'Dejection: An Ode' almost twenty-four years earlier. As part of what I
have called his strategy of recuperation, Coleridge makes his sense of
loss a source of lyric expression, turning what he experiences as personal weakness into poetic strength.

From the time of its first publication in *The Bijou* for 1828 and subsequently in the *Poetical Works* of 1828, 1829, and 1834, 'Work without
Hope' has been one of the few late poems of Coleridge's to be widely
praised. Leigh Hunt, in his critical anthology *Imagination and Fancy*,
wrote:

I insert this poem on account of the exquisite imaginative picture in the third
and fourth lines, and the terseness and melody of the whole. Here we have a
specimen of the perfect style—unsuperfluous, straightforward, suggestive,
and serene.[37]

Yet the poem as Coleridge decided to let us have it, the poem that has so
far been discussed here, is only part of a mixed entry of prose and verse
in Notebook 29, the 'Clasped Vellum Notebook'.[38] In its original state
it has a being similar to that of 'Limbo' and 'Ne Plus Ultra', poems that
can be discussed in themselves, but that can be *fully* discussed only in
relation to their textual matrices.

The Notebook entry begins as a letter dated 21 Feby. 1825 and addressed to 'My dear Friend' (Mrs Anne Gillman). The poet, in beginning, alludes to 'The Eolian Harp of my Brain', thus introducing the
first of several references to the creative principle as represented in
earlier poems. He then develops several images of claustrophobic en-
closure: two mirrors facing each other, a spider's web, windowless
walls. After the fourteen-line poem we know as 'Work without Hope',
these images are further amplified, following a statement of the poet's
method:

> I speak in figures, inward thoughts and woes
> Interpreting by Shapes and outward Shews.

Like the 'Rare Allegories' that Coleridge 'spun' at Christ's Hospital,
the verses that follow convey their meanings in a language of 'Resemb-
lances',[39] or as Coleridge writes in another portion of this Notebook

[37] *Imagination and Fancy*, 214.

[38] I am grateful to the Curator of the Berg Collection, NYPL, for giving me the opportunity to study the Clasped Vellum Notebook and for permission to quote from it. The pertin-
ent text has been published in *CPW* ii. 1110–11, *CL* v. 414–16, and *CN* iv. 5192, and it will
appear in the forthcoming *Poetical Works*, ed. by J. C. C. Mays.

[39] 'Hope and Time', *Poems* 388, l. 9.

entry, 'Thought becomes image and I see it such.' Such preoccupation with the perceived imaginative image was characteristic of the earlier Coleridge, as expressed in his account of the creation of 'Kubla Khan': 'All the images rose up before him as *things*, with a parallel production of consequent expressions' (*CPW* i. 296). Once more, the late Coleridge experiences a renewal of earlier powers.

The rest of the Notebook poem is much worked-over, with at one point ten substitute lines being written on a separate scrap of paper and at another a passage numbering fourteen lines (excluding two deleted ones) being marked as a substitution to be inserted. Taken as a whole, this poetry records a psychic disaster. The poet is enclosed on all sides by the World's 'spidery' thread, and one of the mirrors—the 'Sister Mirror' to that identified as the poet's Faith—'is broke'. Here Coleridge may be remembering Donne's 'The Broken Heart', where 'Love, alas, | At one first blow did shiver it as glass'.[40] Donne's persona is, however, incapacitated but not destroyed: 'Therefore I think my heart hath all | Those pieces still, though they be not unite'; while Coleridge's becomes progressively immured 'With viscous masonry films and threads'. Enclosed in 'a twilight tent' or 'dusky cell', the poet is reminded of 'the nets in Indian Forests found'—an allusion to either the upas-tree or the manchineel.[41] Now completely imprisoned in darkness, the speaker can only bemoan his loss in the intended conclusion:

> I lost my Object and my inmost All—
> Faith *in* the Faith of THE ALONE MOST DEAR!

These lines are signed 'Jacob Hodiernus'—the modern Jacob, linking back to the letter that begins this entry and to the personal drama that led to its composition. Before beginning to indite the verses of 'Work without Hope', Coleridge wrote:

Strain in the manner of G. HERBERT—: which might be entitled THE ALONE MOST DEAR: a Complaint of Jacob to Rachel as in the tenth year of his Service he saw in her ~~and~~ or *fancied* that he saw Symptoms of Alienation.

This is Coleridge's personal code for the situation between himself and Anne Gillman, and she later took an opportunity to write in pencil on

[40] *Poetical Works*, ed. Sir Herbert Grierson (London, 1968), 44.

[41] Kathleen Coburn thinks it is the manchineel, and points out that this poisonous tree is mentioned in line 26 of 'To the Reverend George Coleridge' (*CN* ii. 820 n., *CPW* i. 174, l. 26). The upas tree may be a likelier candidate, but there are botanical difficulties about both: the manchineel grows only in the Western Hemisphere, and the upas tree grows in Java. *Cf.* Blake's use of the latter in *The Book of Ahania*, iii. 69–70, where Urizen 'beheld himself compassed round | And high roofed over with trees' (*Complete Poetry and Prose*, 87).

this page, 'It was fancy.' Presumably she did this at the time that she made a fair copy of 'Work without Hope' for publication. ('Mrs. G. has the Copies—do what you will,' Coleridge says he told James Gillman upon the latter's asking him for previously unpublished poems, including 'Work without Hope', to give to William Pickering for publication in the *Poetical Works* of 1828).[42] To increase the sense of a scriptorial drama going on here, a hand other than Anne Gillman's and possibly Coleridge's has written 'Ah! me!!!' in pen at the bottom of *f* 83v (Berg *f* 170).[43] Coleridge himself may have inscribed these two words after reperusing the manuscript pages.

Considering how much revision had already taken place, the poetry that remained in manuscript, with its finely elaborated conceits, could have been arranged into a complete poem with comparatively little effort. This is in fact what first E. H. Coleridge and then E. L. Griggs did, although the former ignored Coleridge's indication that the eight lines beginning 'Call the World spider: and at Fancy's touch' are not the closing passage but are rather an alternative to the scored-out passage beginning 'Where rising still, still deepning'. A fair copy could have been made up for publication from the working manuscript without much difficulty. This would, of course, have been deeply embarrassing for both Coleridge and the Gillmans, for whatever role-playing may have gone on—'the tenth year of his service' must refer to Coleridge's moving in with the Gillmans in April 1816—the poet was in no position to be a Jacob to Anne Gillman's Rachel. Nor *is* the 'Strain in the manner of G. Herbert', despite the borrowing of the bees-image: the brilliant imagery of the second part might be called post-Metaphysical, but the manner is more reminiscent of Donne, with its drawing-out of multiple conceits, than of Herbert. Finally, and insuperably, the last two lines do not work. At the culmination of what was to be the published 'Work without Hope', Coleridge had succeeded in a most difficult poetic accomplishment—concluding a sonnet (for the published poem really is a sonnet, with unorthodox rhyme and with its sestet preceding its octave) with a generalization. Shakespeare often had the audacity to do

---

[42] Letter to Alaric Watts, 14 Sept. 1828, *CL* vi. 759. The context is Coleridge's explanation of how poems that he had promised to Watts for his annual *The Literary Souvenir* came to be published without Coleridge's consent in Pickering's annual *The Bijou*. See my essay, 'Coleridge and the Annuals', *Huntington Library Quarterly*, 57 (1994), 6–7.

[43] EHC and E. L. Griggs print these words without annotation, presumably accepting them as Coleridge's; Kathleen Coburn (*CN* 5192 n.) is in doubt as to whether the hand is Coleridge's or Mrs Gillman's. In my judgement the hand that wrote 'It was Fancy' did not write 'Ah! me!!!'; the latter could be Coleridge's. It appears to have been written at a different time than the main entry.

this, but the risks are great: sententiousness, banality, bathos. Coleridge must have realized that the second conclusion was a failure that no tinkering could save. 'I lost my Object and my inmost All' is bathetic, and whatever 'THE ALONE MOST DEAR' may have meant to the poet and (possibly) to Anne Gillman, it could mean little to others. In deciding to let the first fourteen lines stand alone and not to publish the rest, Coleridge was once more applying the principle 'that the Più should not overlay the Uno', and despite some memorable passages, the second part of the poem had to be abandoned for the sake of the first. The complex pattern of webs, mirrors, and walls could not have stood without a satisfactory closure; it could only have diminished what Leigh Hunt called the 'terseness and melody of the whole'. Ironically, the consequent artistic success of 'Work without Hope' also had as its by-product the establishment or reconfirmation of the reading public's image of Samuel Taylor Coleridge as a burnt-out case whose poetry declared that he was no longer a poet.

'Lines Suggested by the Last Words of Berengarius'

Most of Coleridge's self-representations involve versions of the poet himself, however fictionalized. An exception is 'Lines Suggested by the Last Words of Berengarius', in which the poet's empathy with his subject is so strong as to make the medieval theologian an aspect of his own identity. In his ninth Philosophical Lecture, Coleridge praised Berengarius of Tours (*c.*1000–88) as one who vainly endeavoured to quell the controversial spirit;[44] and his sympathy is further expressed in a Notebook entry of 1821, where in the course of a long discussion of symbolism and the sacrament he writes of 'the persecution of Berengarius' in connection with disputes about the view of the Eucharist held by 'the Monkish and Papal Faction'. Coleridge continues: 'Berengarius asserts and vindicates the real Presence (and in the same words as our Church Catechism) as earnestly as he rejects the total changes of the corporeal Elements. Thus neither a Sound nor a primary Thought can be a Symbol; but a word may' (*CN* iv. 4831 and n.). The grounds of Coleridge's sympathy for Berengar thus go deeper than the theological question of transubstantiation, important as that was to Coleridge, to the proper understanding of symbolism. The facts that Berengar was silenced by Pope Gregory the Seventh, and that he

---

[44] *Philosophical Lectures*, 272.

attempted to reassert his views only to recant twice, no doubt further
increased Coleridge's identification with his suffering subject. In another Notebook entry, dated 1823–4 by Coburn, Coleridge includes
Berengarius as a man of 'learning and Genius', and quotes from a Latin
poem written by the theologian's disciple, Hildebert of Lawarden, on
his departed master:

> His care was to follow nature, keep the laws:
> To ban sin from his mind, guile from his lips;
> To prefer virtue to wealth, truth to falsehood,
> To say and do nothing without sense . . .
> The envious lament the man they once attacked and hated;
> No less do they now praise and love him . . .
> When I die, may I live and rest with him,
> And may my lot be no better than his.[45]

It may, indeed, have been this Latin poem that first gave Coleridge the
idea of writing his own poem about Berengarius.

Coleridge's source for Hildebert's poem and for much of his other
information about Berengar was W. G. Tennemann's *Geschichte der
Philosophie*[46], and he was also almost certainly familiar with Gotthold
Ephraim Lessing's *Berengarius Turonesis*[47], though, as we shall see, the
verbal influence on his poem comes from a different source. The poem
is conjecturally dated 1826, though it may be that the four lines that
form an introduction to the rest were written a few years earlier,[48] after
Coleridge had read Hildebert's Latin poem in Tennemann. The
'Lines' were published in an annual edited by Coleridge's friend Alaric
Watts, *The Literary Souvenir* for 1827. In the holograph manuscript in
the Huntington Library (HM 12122), the poem begins with
Coleridge's own short 'Testamentary Epitaph' in Greek and Latin; but
Watts wisely reduced this to a footnote, a decision more than endorsed
by the *Poetical Works* of 1828, 1829, and 1834, where it does not appear
at all.[49]

[45] English transl. by Kathleen Coburn, *CN* iv. 5062 n; 6 of these lines appear among
Coleridge's 'Aphorisms on Spiritual Religion', in *Aids to Reflection*, 211–12 n.

[46] (12 vols., Leipzig, 1798–1819), viii. 98–105. Coleridge's copy is in the British Library.

[47] In the edition of Lessing that Coleridge owned (now in the British Library), *Berengarius
Turonesis* is in pt. 13 (1793), 1–211. In some remarks on Thomas Vaughan's *Life and Opinions
of W. de Wycliffe* (London, 1828) in Notebook Q (Berg Collection, NYPL), Coleridge also
refers to what he calls Berengarius's 'mutilated treatise edited by Lessing'. I thank Mary Anne
Perkins for pointing out this reference.

[48] EHC in *CPW* i. 461; J. C. C. Mays in his forthcoming edn. of the *Poetical Works*. The
text cited here is that of the *Literary Souvenir*, with due comparison with the manuscript in
HEH.

[49] These lines were printed separately in *Literary Remains* (1836) and in Sara Coleridge's
edn. of 1844. They appear in *CPW* i. 462 as 'Epitaphium Testamentarium'.

The four lines headed 'Lines | Suggested by the Last Words of Berengarius | Ob. Anno. Dom. 1088' make up a fine, terse, epigrammatic statement.

> No more 'twixt conscience staggering and the Pope;
> Soon shall I now before my God appear,
> By him to be acquitted, as I hope;
> By him to be condemned, as I fear.

As J. C. C. Mays suggests, Coleridge's source here is probably Thomas Fuller's 'The Life and Death of Berengarius': 'Remarkable are his words wherewith he breathed out his last gaspe, which *Illyricus* reporteth to this Effect: *Now as I am to goe, and appeare before God, either to be acquitted by him as I hope, or condemned by him as I feare*.'[50] The first line—'No more 'twixt conscience staggering and the Pope'—is Coleridge's fine invention and deeply colours the tone of the rest. This introduction then leads to the 31-line 'Reflections on the Above'.

Beginning 'Lynx among moles!', the 'Reflections' immediately establishes a sense of intimate presence, as well as making a basic contrast that would have had additional meaning for readers familiar with Coleridge. The lynx, endowed with sharp night vision, is of course contrasted with the blind moles who live in perpetual darkness; but, as we have seen in Chapter 2, for Coleridge the latter had a more particular meaning. It is now the churchmen who persecuted Berengarius who are, in the words of the 1818 *Friend*, 'the partizans of a crass and sensual materialism, the advocates of the Nihil nisi ab extra,' and who

> like moles,
> Nature's mute monks, live mandrakes of the ground,
> Shrink from the light, then listen for a sound;
> See but to dread, and dread they know not why,
> The natural alien of their negative eye.[51]

It is a typical Coleridgean strategy to equate Berengarius's antagonists who believed in literal transubstantiation with empiricists advocating 'Nothing [in the mind] unless from without', as both to him are crass materialists. The poem goes on to converse with the imagined dying theologian in a manner that, as Max Schulz observes, anticipates

---

[50] Mays, Editorial Commentary; Thomas Fuller, *Abel Redevivus / or / The dead yet speaking* (London, 1652), 7. 'The Life and Death of Berengarius' is the first chapter, 1–8. Although Coleridge's copy of *Abel Redevivus* is untraced, among his extant annotated books there are 7 by Fuller, only 2 of which Coleridge dated (1824 and 1829). George Whalley considers the hand 'late' rather than 'early' (*CM* ii. 804).

[51] See *Friend* i. 494 n., *CN* iii. 4073, and the discussion of 'Moles' in Chapter 2 above.

Browning's monologues in its 'use of implied query and explicit re-joinder'.[52] Imagery of darkness and light prevails, much of it adapted from Thomas Fuller; and the animal imagery is extended to the glow-worm (Berengarius) whose 'ray' only serves to guide his enemies, rep-resented as night-birds seeking their prey. Yet this little ray is proleptic of the light that has in increasing degrees now vanquished the darkness. In warning against any feelings of smug superiority towards a pre-decessor who lived in a dark time, Coleridge has in mind Fuller's ad-monition:

This I dare boldly affirme, that if the morning grow so proud so as to scorne the dawning of the day, because mixed with darkness, Midde day will revenge her *Quarrell*, and may justly take the occasion to condemn the Morning, as in lustre inferiour to her selfe.[53]

Thus the poem concludes:

> Yet not for this, if wise, will we decry
> The spots and struggles of the timid DAWN:
> Lest so we tempt the coming NOON to scorn
> The mists and painted vapours of our MORN.

Here Coleridge's sympathetic identification with Berengarius enables him to be both subject and commentator, allowing him to make a de-fence of his own weaknesses in the course of writing an apologia for the medieval theologian whose position on the sacrament anticipated his own.

'The Garden of Boccaccio'

The origin of 'The Garden of Boccaccio' is well-documented. Accord-ing to the Gillmans' grand-daughter, Lucy Watson:

Perceiving one day that the Poet was in a dejected mood, my grandmother silently placed an engraving of this garden on his desk; and the poem was the result. The lines from the eleventh to the sixteenth verses are addressed to her, as my father told me.[54]

While this accords with Coleridge's account in the poem itself, both seem to be masking what was essentially an invitation to a commercial transaction. Frederic Mansell Reynolds, editor of *The Keepsake*, appears to have approached Coleridge for this purpose through the Gillmans. Summer was the time that editors of annuals were most

---

[52] *The Poetic Voices of Coleridge*, 164.   [53] *Abel Redevivus*, 5.
[54] Lucy E. Watson [neé Gillman], *Coleridge At Highgate* (London, 1925), 137.

'The Garden of Boccaccio'

active in soliciting contributions from authors. On 8 August 1828 we find Coleridge inviting Reynolds to take a glass of wine and a sandwich at Highgate and to see the poems he had in 'calligraphic fitness for the Press' (*CL* vi. 749). In September 1828 Coleridge was correcting proof and writing to Reynolds that he was greatly reducing a footnote as had been requested. In the autumn the poem duly appeared in *The Keepsake* for 1829, accompanying an engraving by F. Englehart after Thomas Stothard. Stothard was an artist whose work Coleridge genuinely if not unreservedly admired. 'If it were not for a certain tendency to affectation,' he said, 'scarcely any praise could be too high for Stothard's designs. They give me great pleasure.'[55] The designs Coleridge had in mind were those for Robert Paltock's novel *The Life and Adventures of Peter Wilkins* (1751), which the poet had probably known at Christ's Hospital, for it appeared in *The Novelist's Magazine* with Stothard's illustrations in 1783; but in any event they were republished with the novel in 1816. Coleridge was personally acquainted with the artist, and an engraving by Charles Mottram dated 1815 shows them together with Wordsworth and others at one of Samuel Rogers's breakfasts.[56] The opportunity to write something to accompany one of Stothard's designs must have been an agreeable one for Coleridge.

The picture the poet was shown is unlikely to have been the water colour itself but was probably Englehart's engraving (Fig. 3), as engravings typically preceded the commissioning of texts for annuals. The original, now in the British Museum (Department of Prints and Drawings) is entitled *A Fête Champetre* [*sic*]. Stothard had exhibited a number of paintings on subjects from *The Decameron* at the Royal Academy from 1811 on, in a style that, especially after 1817, was intended to evoke associations of Watteau. These paintings were highly successful,[57] and in 1825 the artist executed ten water-colours based on them. These were engraved by Augustus Fox for the publisher William Pickering, who issued the set of engravings in two forms: as a portfolio entitled *Illustrations of the Decameron of Boccaccio*, and as plates bound into his *Decamerone di Messer Giovanni Boccaccio* (1825). Given his interests both in Italian literature and in the visual arts, Coleridge had probably seen the Fox engraving of this scene, especially as by 1827 arrangements had been made for Pickering to publish his own *Poetical*

55 *Table Talk*, ii. 295 (5 July 1834).
56 For this and other details, see Carl Woodring's note in *Table Talk*, i. 494–5.
57 See Shelley M. Bennett, *Thomas Stothard: The Mechanisms of Art Patronage in England circa 1800* (Columbia, Mo.; University of Missouri Press, 1988), 53–5, 98–9. The drawing on which the *Keepsake* engraving is based is reproduced as Fig. 50.

Works. If so, Coleridge would have appreciated the greater delicacy of Englehart's engraving as well as its higher degree of faithfulness to Boccaccio's text.

The commission, for such it actually was, to write 'The Garden of Boccaccio' stimulated Coleridge in several different ways. The design must have stirred memories of his own experience of the Italian campagna; he may have revisited his description of the landscape of Tuscany in a notebook of 1806; and he may also have reread the relevant part of *The Decameron*, in which Nefile brings the others to the garden on the third day.[58] All three of these elements—direct recollection, Coleridge's notebook text, and the text of *The Decameron*—enter into the composition of 'The Garden of Boccaccio'.

At the beginning of the poem, the poet sits alone in 'A dreary mood', his life empty of 'all genial power', the victim of a 'numbing spell', with a sense of 'my own vacancy' that has left him as a spectator of his feelings—'as I watch'd the dull continuous ache, | which, all else slumbering seem'd alone to wake.' These features have caused critics to make the appropriate comparison of 'Dejection: An Ode',[59] with its sense of vacuity and its failure of genial spirits. At this point, however, the poem takes a turn different from that of 'Dejection', as the poet's discreet muse lays the 'exquisite design' on his desk. Immediately the vocabulary of the poem enters a different realm, with words like 'faery', 'love', 'joyaunce', and 'gallantry', evocative of the fictive world that Coleridge's imagination now enters.[60] Temporarily he regains the sense that he elsewhere calls 'single touch',[61] affording direct access to the world of romance:

[58] Coleridge's admiration of Boccaccio had not in the past extended to *The Decameron*. Herbert G. Wright points out that Coleridge had expressed distaste for it in his lecture of 3 February 1818: *Boccaccio in England from Chaucer to Tennyson* (London: Athlone Press, 1957), 339. In Sept. 1814 Coleridge had tried without success to interest John Murray in a translation of Boccaccio's prose works *excluding* the *Decameron*. See *CL* iii. 529, 562; iv. 570, 592; and Whalley in *CM* i. 542.

[59] See George Whalley, ' "Late Autumn's Amaranth": Coleridge's Late Poems,' 173; George M. Ridenour, 'Source and Allusion in Some Poems of Coleridge', *Studies in Philology*, 60 (1963), 82; Susan Luther, 'The Lost Garden of Coleridge', *TWC* 22 (1992), 25–6.

[60] Jeanie Watson remarks of what she calls his 'symbolic poems of Faery': 'In them Coleridge uses again and again a certain metaphorical cluster of symbols of Spirit: music, androgyny, nature, poetic genius (the symbolic imagination), poetry, the human soul, and Faery', *Risking Enchantment: Coleridge's Symbolic World of Faery* (Lincoln, Nebr., 1990), 55.

[61] Coleridge distinguishes between 'single' and 'double' touch in a number of Notebook entries, such as *CN* ii. 1827. 'Double touch' is associated with volition. It is the adult's manner of apprehending the world, and cannot simply be rejected for the infant's world of single touch. However, temporary access to the latter can be gained through the power of romance. For further discussion of this subject, see John Beer, *Coleridge's Poetic Intelligence* (London and Basingstoke: Macmillan, 1970), 80–9.

> A tremulous warmth crept gradual o'er my chest,
> As though an infant's finger touch'd my breast. (25–6)

Coleridge's manuscript in the Huntington Library shows that something unusual happened at just this this point. A passage was first written in pencil and then a different passage was written in ink over it, partially obliterating it. The first line of the passage was heavily revised. It begins 'A tremulous warmth'—the rest of the line was scored out and the words 'crept gradual o'er my chest' substituted, resulting in line 25 as we have it. Coleridge evidently worked very hard to transmit a key experience here, a stimulus to his imagination that enabled him to make contact with his past identity. This process is embodied once more in a special vocabulary: 'selfless', 'wonder', 'charm'd', 'kindled', 'loved', 'love', and 'lustre'. Much as in his recollection in the *Biographia Literaria* of reading the *Arabian Nights* as a child, Coleridge re-experiences his early response to myth and romance, with evocations of bardic 'Scalds . . . in the sea-worn caves', the Teutonic Hertha[62], and a *Christabel*-like 'minstrel lay, that cheer'd the baron's feast' (39). These fantasy images are not, however, left to inhabit a realm of their own, but are integrated with the reality of Philosophy. For this purpose Coleridge uses in lines 49–56 a slightly different version of a passage that he had originally drafted in the 'Clasped Vellum Notebook' (Berg Collection, NYPL),[63] declaring that Poesy was but Philosophy in an unconscious form and thus known to him from childhood. This gives the poet an opportunity to introduce one of the favourite images of his later poems, that of the child at its mother's knee. The child Poesy has grown up to become the matron Philosophy. Therefore the magical vocabulary that is used to characterize the first—'a faery child' who is

[62] Coleridge mentions Hertha in connection with the mysterious in his 1818 *Lectures on European Literature*; see *Lectures 1808–19* ii. 56, 72, with Tacitus given as a source in the first instance. *Cf. The Complete Works of Tacitus*, trans. Alfred John Church and William Jackson Brodribb (New York; Random House 1942), 728.

[63]
> And there was young Philosophy,
> Unconscious of herself, pardie,
> And now she hight—Poesy—
> And like a child, in life-ful glee,
> Had newly left her Mother's knee,
> Prattles and plays with flower and Stone,
> As if with faery play-fellows
> Revealed to Innocence alone—

There follow some prose and verse not to be found in 'The Garden of Boccaccio', the most notable of which are: 'For Metaphor and Simile | Are notes of lisping prophecy—'; Coburn (*CN* iv. 4623 and n.) dates this entry 1819. It seems likely that the verse was composed with something else in mind than the poem that was eventually written in 1828. A 'variant' of ll. 49–56 printed in *CPW* i. 479 n. is similar to, but not identical with, the Notebook passage.

'with elfin playfellows well known'—can be employed for Philosophy, 'radiant' and 'with no earthly sheen', as well.

In the third division of the poem, the poet has moved from the reverie of the previous part to wakefulness and a sense of mastery as, like Gaston Bachelard's spectator who learns to inhabit an engraving,[64] he declares, 'I see no longer! I myself am there' (65). It is the fusion of art, text, and memory that makes this possible. While it is scarcely possible to distinguish among the three elements at this point, some of their overlapping details are worth considering.

One of the elements that figures prominently in all three is water. Coleridge's Tuscan notebook describes 'The waterfall of Terni' and 'the river Negra meandring thro' it' (*CN* ii. 2849). The Stothard-Englehart illustration gives dramatic prominence to the play of the fountain described in Boccaccio's text:

In the centre of this meadow was a fountain of white marble, beautifully carved . . . and from a figure standing on a column in the midst of the fountain, a jet of water spouted up, which made a most agreeable sound in its fall: the water which came thence ran through the meadow by a secret passage; when, being received into canals, it appeared again and was carried to every part of the garden, uniting into one stream at its going out, and falling with such force into the plain, as to turn two mills before it got thither.[65]

In Coleridge's poem we have water in several manifestations: the nymph's 'restless pool', 'the Tuscan fields and hills, | And famous Arno, fed with all their rills'; and 'many a flower . . . duly fed | With its own rill' (64, 75–6, 88–9).

At other points, too, we see the interplay of details from textual description, picture, and inscribed memory. The arches of the plant-overgrown, aqueduct-like structure in the design must have recalled to Coleridge his walk 'under a pretty arch, half-man half-nature into the orange walk' as well as 'the beautiful bridge of earth over the joined river', which merge in the poem as 'Gardens, where flings the bridge his airy span' (86). On the other hand, 'The golden corn, the olive, and the vine' (79) seem less related to anything in either Boccaccio's account or the design than to Coleridge's own walk in 1806: 'through the vineyard, small fields of wheat, vines & olive Trees | Corn, Wine Oil!' becomes 'The golden corn, the olive, and the vine' (80). Then, in the last part of the poem, both *ekphrasis* and recollection are abandoned in favour of the poet's own invention, first in his depiction of Boccaccio in lines 97–100

---

[64] *The Poetics of Space*, trans. Marie Jolas (New York: Orion Press, 1964), 50.
[65] *The Decameron*, trans. W. K. Kelley (London, 1855), 135.

and the accompanying footnote, and then in his concluding self-presentation.

In lines 97–100 the poet draws our attention to the figure of Boccaccio, who is, of course, not in the picture but has been placed there by the poet. The author is seen 'unfolding on his knees | The new-found roll of old Maeonides'; but with Ovid's *Ars Amoris* closer to his heart. Susan Luther astutely observes that ' "Boccace" . . . metonymically figures S. T. Coleridge, the present ideal, great reader who "unfolds" the text.'[66] In his own note to this passage, printed in *The Keepsake* with the poem, Coleridge passes from the *Decameron* to the *Filocopo*, 'where the sage instructor, Racheo, as soon as the young prince and the beautiful girl Biancofiore had learned their letters, sets them to study the Holy Book, Ovid's Art of Love' (*CPW* i. 480n. 2.). Having identified himself with Boccaccio as a conveyor of the tradition of courtly love, Coleridge now becomes the reader of an erotic text as well as the inhabitant of an engraving:

> Long may it be mine to con thy mazy page,
> Where half conceal'd, the eye of fancy views
> Fauns, nymphs, and wingèd saints, all gracious to thy muse!
>
> (102–4)

The introduction of the word 'mazy' brings in associations with both the 'mazy motion' of the sacred river in 'Kubla Khan' and, with a slight attendant ambiguity, Milton's description of Paradise:

> Brooks,
> Rolling on Orient Pearl and sands of Gold,
> With mazy error under pendant shades
> Ran Nectar, visiting each plant . . .
>
> (*Paradise Lost* iv. 237–40)

Although Coleridge elsewhere insisted, 'The *holy book*—Ovid's Art of Love!! This is not the result of mere Immorality',[67] a persistent element of erotic fantasy pervades the poet's depiction of himself as a voyeur watching nymphs and associated with 'that sly satyr peeping through the leaves!' in the last line. Despite Coleridge's use of the demonstrative adjective, which suggests that we have returned to the picture, there is no satyr in either Stothard's drawing or the engravings after it. That satyr is an invention of the sly poet, like Eliot's Mr Apollinax or the namesake of one of Coleridge's alter egos, Satyrane.

---

[66] 'The Lost Garden of Coleridge', 28.
[67] Note about the passage from *Il Filocopo* quoted above, written by Coleridge in his copy of Boccaccio's *Opere*; see *CPW* i. 480 n. 2, and *CM* i. 544.

As we have seen, Coleridge's own self-representation is an important subject in his poetry of the 1820s. The characteristics of the self that are represented are, of course, carefully selected. Conscious of his physical decay, out of harmony with the goings-on of the natural world, misunderstood by his contemporaries, yet still able to produce poetry when stimulated by memory, this fictive self is a figure combining wisdom with pathos. This is nowhere so evident as in some of the most personal of Coleridge's later poems—poems about love, or, more precisely, about the absence of love and the coping strategies that make that absence bearable.

4 LOVE

Love was always an important theme in Coleridge's poetry, and the beautiful 'Recollections of Love', begun after a return to the Quantock Hills in 1807, shows that he retained the capacity for lyric evocation. Especially touching is the identification of 'Love's whisper' with the sound of the Greta that concludes the poem:

> Sole voice, when other voices sleep,
> Dear under-song in clamor's hour.
> (*CPW* i. 410).

More frequently, however, in Coleridge's later poetry love is a threatening force or an aching void. Recognizing this, in the editions of his *Poetical Works* published in his lifetime, the poet introduced the section containing most of his later poems[1] with a four-line motto bearing the Greek title 'Love, always a talkative companion':

> In many ways does the full heart reveal
> The presence of the love it would conceal;
> But in far more th' estrangèd heart lets know
> The absence of the love, which yet it fain would show.
> (*CPW* i. 462)

The theme of disjunction in the epigram is at the same time intensified by its extra-metrical last line and (at least partially) undermined by the ironical title. By choosing this as a motto Coleridge both calls attention to the prominence of love as a subject in his later poetry and thematizes its absence.

In some of what have come to be known as the 'Asra' poems, thanks to George Whalley's excellent *Coleridge and Sara Hutchinson*, Coleridge's expression of unfulfilled feeling is bitterly direct. This is true of 'Separation', for which Coleridge wrote a memorable new beginning some time after the draft in one of his Notebooks:

---

[1] As noted in the Introduction, the title of this section was changed in 1834 from 'Prose in Rhyme; and Epigrams, Moralities, and Things without a Name' to 'Miscellaneous Poems'. In *The Poems of Samuel Taylor Coleridge*, ed. Sara Coleridge and Derwent Coleridge (London, 1852) it was changed again, to the more appropriate 'Poems written in Later Life'.

> A sworded man whose trade is blood,
>   In grief, in anger, and in fear,
> Thro' jungle, swamp, and torrent flood,
>   I seek the wealth you hold so dear![2]

This is a startling parallel to a poem Coleridge could not have read, William Blake's Notebook poem beginning 'My Spectre around me night & Day' (*E* 475–7), in which 'He scents thy footsteps in the snow | Wheresoever thou dost go.' In Blakean terms, Coleridge's speaker is a hungry, ravening Spectre, forever incomplete without his Emanation or female counterpart. Without the added first stanza, Coleridge's lyric is a naked confession of emotional need that collapses into an eight-line borrowing from Charles Cotton's 'Chlorinda'. Another Asra lyric also closes anticlimactically after a strong beginning:

> Song
>
> Though veiled in spires of myrtle-wreath,
> Love is a sword which cuts its sheath,
> And through the clefts itself has made,
> We spy the flashes of the blade![3]

Borrowing the trope of sword and sheath from Byron's famous lyric, Coleridge turns it to other purposes—not the elegiac world-weariness of 'So we'll go no more a-roving', but a bitter statement that the myrtle, emblematic of marriage, hides the self-destructive qualities of love. Yet the successor to this memorable quatrain falters, first virtually repeating lines 3 and 4 and then concluding awkwardly with an image of impotence:

> But through the clefts itself has made,
> We likewise see Love's flashing blade,
> By rust consumed, or snapt in twain;
> And only hilt and stump remain.

We may infer that Coleridge was dissatisfied with both these poems: 'Song' appeared only in the *Poetical Works* of 1828, while 'Separation' was published only in the edition of 1834, which Henry Nelson Coleridge was chiefly responsible for editing.

Another attempt to deal with the destructive power of love was through the mediated discourse of narrative. Coleridge's most ambitious attempt in this mode in his later years was 'Alice Du Clos',

---

[2] *CPW* i. 397. EHC dates the Notebook draft from the Malta period and the whole poem ?1805; Beer, *Poems* (rev. edn., London, 1993), 416, dates the draft version ?1809–10.

[3] *CPW* i. 450–51. Undated.

completed in 1829, though he used some fragmentary earlier Notebook verses (*CN* i. 1066, ii. 1915, iii. 4163) in it. In a letter to the editor of *The Keepsake*, Frederic M. Reynolds, Coleridge refers to the poem as a 'Lyrical Ballad', thus harking back to his most creative period.[4] It is indeed an ambitious poem, 193 lines long, telling a story of the brutal effects of jealousy. Alice Du Clos is engaged to Lord Julian, 'a hasty man' (1. 78). His vassal, Sir Hugh, comes to summon her to go hunting and finds her, as if at the end of 'The Garden of Boccaccio', in her bower 'conning then | Don Ovid's mazy tale of loves' (35–6). Sir Hugh, with a pun that reveals or should reveal his duplicity, reports that her eyes were 'fix'd with steadfast gaze | Full on her wanton page' (168–9). In an odd reversal of the situation in 'Time, Real and Imaginary', the youth 'with reverted face doth ride' ahead of her to meet Lord Julian. Believing the perfidious Sir Hugh, Lord Julian hurls his javelin at Alice, leaving her 'bleeding on the glade' (193). The flashes of love's blade have been seen again, with a tragic result.

Coleridge blamed his inability to write an appropriate conclusion for 'Alice Du Clos' on the emotional effects of a dispute with Frederic Reynolds about the payment for 'The Garden of Boccaccio' and some short poems published in *The Keepsake* for 1829.[5] 'It was my original intention,' Coleridge wrote, 'to have annexed as a sort of Post-script Super-conclusion from six to eight stanzas in the legendary, supernatural, imaginative style of popular superstition' (July 1829, *CL* vi. 800). On 6 August he continued:

Besides, I had from the first planning of the Ballad conceived & intended what struck me as a highly lyrical & impressive conclusion—intimating the fate & punishment of Julian the Traitor—and tho' every thought & image is present to my mind, I have not the power of bringing them forth in the requisite force & fire of diction & metre. For Poetry (if any thing I write, can deserve that name) is surely not a matter of will or choice with me. That *sickish* Feel, that is sure to accompany the attempt to compose verses mechanically, by dint of the head alone, acts like a poison on my health. (*CL* vi. 808)

It is clear that Coleridge had a high regard for 'Alice Du Clos' and had put considerable work into it. Yet it is hard to see how the supernatural punishment of Frederic would have worked in a poem that had done without the supernatural for nearly two hundred lines. In the end the ballad was withdrawn from *The Keepsake* and first published in the *Poetical Works* of 1834.

---

[4] Letter of July 1829; see *CL* vi. 800.

[5] For details see my 'Coleridge and the Annuals', *Huntington Library Quarterly*, 57 (1994), 1–24.

Coleridge's artistically successful late poems about love are those in which he uses aspects of the persona developed in the poems discussed in Chapter 3. Such personae do not, in contrast with Yeats's masks, constitute antithetical selves. They are, rather, simplified exaggerations of the poet's subjectivity, through which he can present painful aspects of his existence in verbal constructions that remain under his control. Using such enabling fictions, he can assume a variety of stances. He can be the wise but slightly comical Improvisatore who has renounced love for friendship, the concerned family friend of 'The Two Founts' who appears not to notice that he is at the brink of infatuation, the weaver of a bitter allegory in 'The Pang More Sharp Than All', the speculative philosopher of 'Constancy to an Ideal Object', or the devastated spectator of 'Love's Apparition and Evanishment'. Whether or not such strategies gave Coleridge the emotional compensation he sometimes claimed to have realized, they made it possible for him to make poetry, some of it of exceptional interest, out of his most personal feelings.

'The Improvisatore'

If reprinted without its prose matrix, 'The Improvisatore' may seem an example of self-pity, lacking in dignity.[6] However, the prose, as Coleridge indicated by publishing it with the poem in the *Poetical Works* of 1829, is an essential part of the work; it not only introduces the poem but also provides a perspective upon its major figure through his dialogue with his young friends:

KATHERINE. . . . But is there any such true love?
FRIEND. I hope so.
KATH. But do you believe it?
ELIZABETH. (*eagerly*). I am sure he does.
FRI. From a man turned of fifty, Katherine, I imagine, expects a less confident answer.
KATH. A more sincere one, perhaps.
FRI. Even though he should have obtained the nick-name of Improvisatore by perpetrating charades and extempore verses at Christmas times?[7]

---

[6] See e.g. Schulz, *The Poetic Voices of Coleridge* (Detroit, 1963), 164.

[7] *CPW* i. 463. *The Improvisatore* was first published in the *Amulet* for 1828 with a prose preamble called 'New Thoughts on Old Subjects;/ Or Conversational Dialogues on Interests and Events of Common Life.' Here Coleridge proposed a series of further contributions to come. These were not realized, and Coleridge did not reprint the preamble (as distinguished

The Improvisatore is sketched as a figure both wise and slightly ridiculous, something like Drosselmeyer, who in the ballet *The Nutcracker* provides the magic but has only a walking part. And although Coleridge was not literally an improvisatore performer, the idea of improvisation had great appeal for him, as witnessed by 'Aria Spontanea' (the original title of the first-written part of 'Youth and Age') and the lovely 'Song, *ex improviso*' (*CPW* i. 483), first published in *The Keepsake* for 1830. John Taylor Coleridge wrote in June 1825 after a visit from his uncle: 'He is a real improvisatore on *every* subject and a quack in none.'[8] His manner of reciting his own poetry also had improvisatore-like qualities as Henry Nelson Coleridge described it:

not rhetorical, but musical, so very near recitative that for any one else to attempt it would be ridiculous, and yet it is perfectly miraculous with what exquisite searching he elicits and makes sensible every particular of the meanings, not leaving a shadow of the feeling, the mood, the degree untouched.[9]

Coleridge's interest in improvisation was shared by other authors of the 1820s and presumably by their audiences as well; parallels have been pointed out in works by Letitia Elizabeth Landon, Winthrop Mackworth Praed, and Thomas Lovell Beddoes.[10]

The poem 'extemporized' by 'The Friend' has as its theme the renunciation of love, which is figured in terms of food and drink and also, in a variation of the image in 'Work without Hope', as 'Late autumn's Amaranth, that more fragrant blows | When Passion's flowers all fall or fade' (ll. 56–7). The poet once thought he possessed love, which was 'Crown of his cup and garnish of his dish' (5). However, the expected nourishment was not forthcoming, and there follows one of Coleridge's little dramas involving personifications: Fancy, unfed, lies sick, 'Telling her dreams to jealous Fear!' (40), until the Poet relinquishes Hope. This act also involves giving up speculation on the nature of

---

from the prose of 'The Improvisatore' itself). Otherwise, the text for the *Poetical Works* of 1829 was set from the copy used for *The Amulet*. In January 1829 Coleridge wrote to William Pickering asking him to take all possible care that Mrs Gillman's copy of *The Amulet* not be spoiled and saying that 'The part to be reprinted begins on p. 39, and concludes on p. 47.' See Eric W. Nye, 'Coleridge and the Publishers: Twelve New Manuscripts', *Modern Philology*, 87 (1989), 66.

[8] Quoted by Carl Woodring, Introduction to *Table Talk* i. p. li.

[9] Reprinted from the *Quarterly Review* (1834) in *Coleridge: The Critical Heritage*, ed. J. de G. Jackson (London: Routledge & Kegan Paul, 1971), 627.

[10] Schulz, *The Poetic Voices of Coleridge*, 156–8, calls attention to considerable contemporary interest in improvization: the hero of Praed's *The Troubadour* (1823–4), the heroine of Letitia Landon's *The Improvisatore* (1824), and the provider of narrative unity to collections of stories like Beddoes's *The Improvisatore* and Landon's *The Golden Violet* (1827).

Love, which is what the Improvisatore has been asked his opinion
about. Using imagery very close to that of 'Constancy to an Ideal
Object' (see below), he abandons the question with 'If this were ever
his, in outward being, | Or but his own true love's projected shade'
(58–9). The Amaranth, carried by Adam and Eve from Eden, outlast-
ing 'Passion's flowers', may once have been his but is no longer. As in
'Work without Hope', Coleridge appears indebted to Charlotte Smith
here, perhaps to a different poem, 'Thirty-Eight':

> Tho' Time's inexorable sway,
> Has torn the myrtle bands away,
> For other wreaths 'tis not too late,
> The amaranth's purple glow survives . . .[11]

Katherine, Elizabeth, and Lucius would no doubt have preferred a different answer, an answer of the sort provided by Coleridge himself in
his poem 'To Mary Pridham', in which he uses three (juxtaposed) lines
of the 'Answer, *ex improviso*' to create a far different message for the
woman his son was about to marry:

> Now I revive, Hope making a new start,
> Since I have heard with most believing heart,
> That all my glad eyes would grow bright to see,
> My Derwent hath found realiz'd in thee,
> The boon prefigur'd in his earliest wish
> Crown of his cup and garnish of his dish![12]

Coleridge believed not that the fulfilment of love was impossible, but
that it was impossible for him. The 'Answer, *ex improviso*' records his
conviction about his own life and claims a compensatory tranquillity. It
exhibits some of the characteristics that George Whalley assigns
to what he calls Coleridge's 'emblem poems', including 'heraldic
specificity' and 'a strong gnomic or moral emphasis'. Although the
Improvisatore does not give his fictional audience the answer it might
wish, creating this figure gives Coleridge an opportunity to make a personal statement through the use of a persona. Other late poems about
love employ variants of this poetic strategy, using the first person
singular in such a way as to achieve a sense of control over the subject
matter.
    A poem in which Coleridge exhibits this ability with considerable
lightness of touch is 'The Two Founts'. A poem of friendship rather

---

[11] *Elegiac Sonnets* (7th edn., London, 1795), 84.
[12] 'To Mary Pridham', 16 Oct. 1827, *CPW* i. 468.

than love, 'The Two Founts' seems at times about to cross the boundary from one to the other. It was written in 1826 for Mrs Eliza Aders, wife of the banker and art collector Charles Aders and daughter of the well-known engraver Raphael Smith. A cultivated and beautiful woman, Mrs Aders held gatherings on Euston Square that attracted some of the best known cultural figures of the age. If the story of a meeting between Coleridge and William Blake is true, one of the Aders's evenings would be the most likely place, as visits by each are documented.[13] The germ of the poem is in a Notebook entry of May 1826 (*CN* iv. 5368), in four of eight lines of verse headed 'A.G.'. If the poem was originally meant for Anne Gillman, this would be another instance of Coleridge's well-known capacity for substituting one idealized woman for another. However, it may well be that the heading 'A.G.' refers to Mrs Gillman's remark concerning Mrs Aders's bearing her 'intense Suffering', mentioned by Coleridge in the letter that he sent to Mrs Aders with the poem, here called 'To Eliza in Pain' (3 June 1826, *CL* vi. 581–3; see also 662–5). I shall, however, refer to it by the title Coleridge gave it in his *Poetical Works* of 1828.

The central conceit of 'The Two Founts' is that the poet is visited by a Dwarf from Dreamland who informs him that in every heart 'Two Founts there are, of Suffering and Cheer!'.[14] This idea of a double source was deeply ingrained in Coleridge's mind, going back at least to the 'twy-streaming fount' of Property in *Religious Musings* (line 204). Eliza alone has been allowed to unlock only one of the two, and 'Of Pleasure only will to all dispense'. The 'stern | and torturing Genius of the bitter spring' is compelled 'To shrink aback, and cower upon his urn'. However, there is an equal and opposite reaction as 'The Fount of Pain | O'erflowing beats against its lovely mound', causing 'wild flashes' (presumably migraines) to shoot from heart to brain. Therefore the poet urges Eliza to be 'less good, less sweet, less wise!' Whatever the psychological wisdom of such advice may be, there seems little hope that Eliza can take it, as she has been presented as a *schöne Seele* who can do no other. As for the Dwarf, he seems, with 'his raised lip, that aped a critic smile' more of an emissary from the *Edinburgh Review* than from Dreamland. At the same time, there is a powerful erotic undercurrent that has little to do with the poem's ostensible subject. Eliza is compared

[13] See Alexander Gilchrist, *The Life of William Blake*, ed. Ruthven Todd (2nd edn. London: J. M. Dent, 1945), 331–2.

[14] A variant of the two opening lines is written on the dedication page of vol. ii of Coleridge's copy of *Mesmerismus* by Christian Wolfart (Berlin, 1815) in the British Library. Evidently the poet at some point associated the subject of the poem with a Mesmeric cure.

to a rainbow, which in turn is troped to 'a bridge to tempt the angels down'. In the subtitle the reader is informed that the Lady has recovered '*with unblemished looks*' (emphasis mine). One manuscript stanza may have been cancelled because it went too far in praising the appearance of another man's wife:

> Was ne'er on earth seen beauty like to this,
>   A concentrated satisfying sight!
> In its deep quiet, ask no further bliss—
> At once the form and substance of delight.[15]

'The Two Founts', though an occasional poem, exhibits some of the characteristics of Coleridge's more ambitious later poetry. It is personal in subject, intimate in tone, and suffused with thinly disguised eroticism. It employs allegory as a central device, 'faery' subject matter, and personification. And one further feature is of some importance: it was widely disseminated. Before appearing in the *Poetical Works* of 1828 and the subsequent two lifetime collections, it was published in *The Bijou* for 1828 (which, like other Annuals, appeared in the autumn of the year preceding its cover date) and was reprinted in *The Annual Register* for 1827 and in the *Monthly Repository* for 1827. Like a number of other late poems, it reached a very large reading public.

'Constancy to an Ideal Object' displays some of the features of 'The Two Founts', but on a deeper and more probing level. The date of this poem is uncertain. E. H. Coleridge conjecturally dated it '?1826', but James Dykes Campbell believed that, because of line 18—'To have a home, an English home, and thee!'—it must have been written at Malta *c*. 1805.[16] It should also be noted that on 11 June 1825 Coleridge wrote to J. H. Green, 'Could you procure me a Copy of those Lines which a long time ago I sent to Mrs. Green by you, on constancy to the *Idea* of a beloved Object—ending, I remember, with the Simile of a Woodman following his own projected Shadow?' (*CL* v. 467). We do not, of course, know what Coleridge meant by 'a long time', but Coleridge became acquainted with Green only in 1817. If anything, this suggests that the poem was not finished at the time that *Sibylline Leaves* went to press. As we have seen, Coleridge was eager to include in that volume as much of his poetry as he could, but 'Constancy to an Ideal Object' was not published until the *Poetical Works* of 1828. The argument for a relatively early date rests entirely on the assumptions that Coleridge could specify 'an English home' only if he were not in England at the time and that

---

[15] *CPW* i. 454 n. These lines are not included in the holograph MS in the Berg Collection of the New York Public Library.   [16] *CPW* i. 456; *JDC* 635.

the entire poem must have been written at the same time as line 17. Coleridge's interest in the phenomenon of the 'Brocken Spectre' was virtually lifelong, and so cannot help to date the poem; but his most striking poetic use of the image, with a significance very similar to that in this poem, occurs in 'The Improvisatore':

> If this were ever his, in outward being,
> Or but his own true love's projected shade [.]
>
> *(CPW* i. 468, 58–9).

In the absence of physical evidence, 'Constancy to an Ideal Object' cannot be dated precisely, but it appears almost certain that it belongs among Coleridge's later poetry. That it is one of his most important poems on the subject of love is indisputable.

The poem begins with the poet's direct address to the internalized image, or imago, of his beloved.

> Since all that beat about in Nature's range,
> Or veer or vanish; why should'st thou remain
> The only constant in a world of change,
> O yearning Thought! that liv'st but in the brain?

The peculiar words 'beat about' suggest birds flying in the field of vision that is 'Nature's range', only to move out of sight. The opposition between these mere phenomena and 'Thought' is something like that between 'Fish, flesh, and fowl' and 'Monuments of unaging intellect' in Yeats's 'Sailing to Byzantium'—but more tentative, as the poet questions whether the world of thought may be mutable too.

> Call to the Hours, that in the distance play,
> The faery people of the future day——
> Fond Thought! not one of all that shining swarm
> Will breathe on thee with life-enkindling breath,
> Till when, like strangers shelt'ring from a storm,
> Hope and Despair meet in the porch of Death!

Bringing in 'faery' puts a special emphasis on what I. A. Richards accurately glossed as 'these anticipations—these endless dreams of future fulfillment'.[17] Time-not-yet-existing seems magical, but it cannot bring Thought to life in our physical existence. The personifications of Hope and Despair occur, as has already been discussed, in the third paragraph of Coleridge's 'Allegoric Vision' (first published with the *Lay Sermon* of 1817): 'Like two strangers that have fled to the same

---

[17] *Coleridge's Minor Poems* (n.p.: Folcroft Press, 1970 [1960]), 22–3.

shelter from the same storm, not seldom do Despair and Hope meet for the first time in the porch of Death!'[18]

This desperate thought leads to a further address to the imago:

> Yet still thou haunt'st me; and though well I see,
> She is not thou, and only thou art she.

This is very much in the vein of a poem Coleridge certainly knew, Donne's Elegy X, 'The Dream', which begins with a similar paradox expressed in direct address:

> *Image* of her whom I love, more than she,
> Whose fair impression in my faithful heart[19]

As in Donne's poem, Coleridge recognizes that the image has become an eidolon, contemplated

> Still, still as though some dear embodied Good,
> Some living love before my eyes there stood.

Coleridge's attitude also has much in common with the love-psychology encountered in early Italian poetry among the poets of the *dolce stil novo*. For evidence of this, we may turn for a moment to the beautiful little poem called 'First Advent of Love', which begins 'O fair is Love's first hope to gentle mind' (*CPW* i. 443). It has been pointed out that this line is virtually a translation of the first line of Guido Guinicelli's canzone 'Al cor gentil ripara sempre Amore'.[20] Another indication of Coleridge's knowledge of this subject is the fragment published by E. H. Coleridge as 'Questions and Answers in the Court of Love' (*CPW* ii. 1109). This begins with a typical courtly love trope, in the form of the question 'Why is my Love like the Sun?' There follow analogies between love and four times of day, including five lines published in slightly different form in the beautiful lyric 'Recollections of Love' (*CPW* i. 409). We may assume that Coleridge knew the love-psychology of stilnovistic poems in which an image of the beloved woman crystallizes in the lover's heart and is worshipped there as in a shrine.

Despite these striking similarities, the solutions adopted by Guinicelli and his circle, and by Donne, are not embraced in 'Constancy

---

[18] *JDC* 635; *Lay Sermons* 133; see above, p. 35.

[19] *Poetical Works*, ed. Sir Herbert Grierson (London: Oxford University Press, 1968 [1933]), 84–5.

[20] George Ridenour, 'Source and Allusion in Some Poems of Coleridge', *Studies in Philology*, 60 (1963), 76–7. EHC (*CPW* i. 443 n.) points out that although Coleridge referred to 'First Advent of Love' as composed before his fifteenth year, it appears to originate in a Notebook entry of 1824.

to an Ideal Object'. The secularization of the sacred, the worship of the imago as a saint that forms part of the ethos of the *dolce stil novo*, is too rooted in the conventions and typologies of late medieval culture to be available to Coleridge. Donne is closer in presenting the love of the eidolon as a problem rather than an ethos; yet the jaunty paradox in which he blithely casts aside the knowability or unknowability of the love object—'So, if I dreame I have you, I have you, | For all our joys are but fantasticall'—and abandons himself to being 'mad with much *heart*' is not a Coleridgean solution. For Coleridge, such ambiguity is a source of anguish. At first he indulges in a fantasy of domesticity deeply rooted in his earlier poetry and embodied in the image of the 'cot', as at the end of 'The Eolian Harp', where the poet possesses 'PEACE, and this COT, and THEE, heart-honor'd Maid!' In Coleridge's poetry of the 1790s the Cot represents the domestic microcosm of a millennial society.[21] In 'Constancy to an Ideal Object' it is recognized as a wish-fulfilment fantasy that gives way, as has often been noted, to another sort of image from Coleridge's poetry of the 1790s:

> The peacefull'st cot the moon shall shine upon,
> Lull'd by the thrush and wakened by the lark,
> Without thee were but a becalmèd bark,
> Whose Helmsman on an ocean waste and wide
> Sits mute and pale his mouldering helm beside.

The self-referentiality that often characterizes the later poems is here projected in a double aspect, the implication being that if the first possibility—Coleridge as possessor of Cot and Maid—turns out to be untenable, the only alternative is the second: Coleridge as the Ancient Mariner.

The dilemma is summed up in the last eight lines, beginning with the question 'And art though nothing?' and proceeding to the comparison of the Brocken Spectre. Coleridge's interest in this phenomenon was almost obsessional, and he refers to it frequently. We should, however, be be aware that the meaning given to this image in Coleridge's prose differs according to context, and what we find in his various discussions of it is a spectrum of possible meanings.

Coleridge was of course aware of the optical nature of the phenomenon. In a MS note to his own *Aids to Reflection*, he wrote:

This refers to a curious phænomenon, which occurs occasionally when the Air is filled with fine particles of frozen Snow, constituting an almost invisibly subtle Snow-mist, and a person is walking with the Sun behind his Back. His

---

[21] See my 'Apocalypse and Millennium in the Poetry of Coleridge', *TWC* 23 (1992), 24–34.

shadow is projected, and he seems a figure moving before him with a glory round its Head. I have myself seen it twice: and it is described in the first or second Volume of the Manchester Philosophical Transactions.[22]

In Coleridge's source the image is seen on a mountain above the Valley of Clwyd:

—In the road above me, I was struck with the peculiar appearance of a very white shining cloud that lay remarkably close to the ground. The Sun was nearly setting but shone extremely bright. I walked up to the cloud, and my shadow was projected into it; the head of my shadow was surrounded at some distance by a circle of various colours whose centre appeared to be near the situation of the eye, and whose circumference extended to my shoulders. The circle was complete except where the shadow of my body intercepted it—it exhibited the most vivid colors, red being outermost—all the colors appeared in the same order and proportion that the rainbow presents to our view.[23]

In one of his Notebooks, Coleridge also copied out a German account published in 1798:

In this mist, when the sun had risen, I could see my shadow, a gigantic size, for a few seconds moving as I moved, but then I was swiftly enveloped in mist, and the apparition was gone. When the sun reaches a higher position than that where its rays fall directly upon us, it is impossible to observe this phenomenon, because at any higher position of the sun our shadow is cast below us rather than in front of us. . . . Just after a quarter past four I walked towards the inn . . . And behold! I saw, towards the Achtermannshöhe, at a great distance, a human form of gigantic size . . . I cannot describe my joy at this discovery; for I had taken so many blessed steps in vain in pursuit of this phantom and had never been able to lay hold of it.[24]

Coleridge made literary use of this image, both with reference to his own works and to those of others. In the ninth of his lectures on Shakespeare and Milton of 1811–12, he remarks: 'The reader often feels that some ideal trait of our own is caught or some nerve has been touched of which we were not before aware and it is proved that it has been touched by the vibration that we feel a sort of thrilling which tells us that we know ourselves the better for it.'[25] He then makes an analogy with the Brocken Spectre:

[22] *Aids to Reflection*, 227 n. In another of the annotated copies cited by Beer, Coleridge uses the expression 'a Painter's Glory'.

[23] *The Road to Xanadu* (London; Constable, 1927), 470–1 n. 138, from 'Description of a Glory' by John Haygarth, in *Memoirs of the Literary and Philosophical Society of Manchester*, 3 (1790), 463–7. Lowes observes that Coleridge borrowed this volume from the Bristol Library in 1798.

[24] *CN* i. 430 3½. 40 n. From 'Beobachtung des Brokengespenstes', mittgetheilt von J. Lud. Jordan, *Göttingisches Journal der Naturwissenschaften*, ed. J. Fr. Gmelin, 1/iii (1798), 110–14.

[25] *Lectures 1808–19 on Literature* i. 352 (deletions omitted).

In the plays of Shakespeare every man sees himself without knowing that he sees himself as in the phenomena of nature, in the mist of the mountains a traveller beholds his own figure but the glory round the head distinguishes it from a mere vulgar copy; or as a man traversing the Brocken in the north of Germany at sunrise when the glorious beams are shot ascance the mountain: he sees before him a figure of such elevated dignity, that he only knows it to be himself by the similarity of action.

Shakespeare's meaning is to be found within the reader's own being, just as the figure with a glory round its head must be recognized as a self-projection. Similarly, in the printed passage in *Aids to Reflection* (227) to which he added the note already cited, Coleridge makes the Spectre a trope for Genius:

Pindar's remark on sweet Music holds equally true of Genius: as many as are not delighted by it are disturbed, perplexed, irritated. The Beholder either recognizes it as a projected Form of his own Being, that moves before him with a Glory round its head, or recoils from it as from a Spectre.

At first this image may seem neutral in value, as it is for the 'beholder' to invest it with meaning. Yet it must be said that the beholder who recoils from Genius as from a spectre seems less interesting than the one who recognizes it as a projected form of his own being. If we were to regard Coleridge's other uses of the analogy, we would find further seeming inconsistencies—I say 'seeming' because it is in the very nature of this image to have more than one meaning. Each time he recontextualizes this image Coleridge revalorizes it.

This being so, it is not surprising that 'Constancy to an Ideal Object' has been subjected to contrasting critical interpretations. It can be viewed very pessimistically, with the image of the glory regarded as 'the self-generated illusion of the rustic'.[26] Or, contrastingly, the rustic's activity may be viewed positively: 'He pursues, and *by his own act of pursuit* gives life to his ideal.'[27] The pursuit may be seen as a correlative to the poetic enterprise: 'Through the "life-enkindling" power of the poet's imagination, his abstractions are reclaimed from pure thought and returned to the life that fostered them.'[28] Closer to my own view is that of Tilottama Rajan, for whom this poem 'recognizes both love's apparition and its evanishment, and achieves the difficult peace which eluded Coleridge in his poem of that name'; at the same time, Rajan

[26] James T. Boulger, *Coleridge As Religious Thinker* (New Haven: Yale University Press, 1961), 209–10.

[27] Stephen Prickett, *Coleridge and Wordsworth: The Poetry of Growth* (Cambridge: Cambridge University Press, 1970), 22–3.

[28] Edward Kessler, *Coleridge's Metaphors of Being* (Princeton, NJ, 1979), 136.

underscores 'the ironic element which continues to complicate the constitutive power of imagination even at the end'.[29] Something further needs to be said about that end, however, and about the two literal descriptions of the phenomenon cited earlier.

Following the question 'And art thou nothing?' Coleridge gives an analogy that seems to be the answer but that is itself, as we have seen, subject to interpretation.

> Such thou art, as when
> The woodman winding westward up the glen
> At wintry dawn, where o'er the sheep-track's haze,
> Sees full before him, gliding without tread,
> An image with a glory round its head;
> The enamoured rustic worships its fair hues,
> Nor knows he makes the shadow, he pursues!

In the two accounts to which we know Coleridge was indebted, the narrator does not find anything supernatural in the image. John Haygarth is motivated by scientific interest, but is not oblivious to the visual beauty of the phenomenon, as his description of its rainbow colours attests. J. Lud. Jordan is actuated more by mere curiosity, but he too is under no illusion, and his response is one of gratification: 'I cannot describe my joy at this discovery; for I had taken so many blessed steps in vain in pursuit of this phantom and had never been able to lay hold of it.' With these two, Samuel Taylor Coleridge makes a third. He too is sensible of the beauty of the scene—'The viewless snow-mist weaves a glist'ning haze' is reminiscent of imagery associated with the imagination in poems of the 1790s, as, for example, the mist, cloud, and fogsmoke white, through which the Albatross was seen in 'The Rime of the Ancient Mariner'. The poet is distinguished from the woodman, who believes in the literal reality of the apparition and worships it without knowing its source; like the two observers upon whose accounts he drew, he knows the source and can take pleasure in the phenomenon without being deluded by it. There remains a certain poignancy in his knowledge that the image is self-generated. That self-knowledge brings freedom from illusion but not emotional fulfilment is a theme of the later poems.

The question of the reality of love is also at the centre, though in a much different way, of 'The Pang More Sharp Than All'. First published in the *Poetical Works* of 1834 (where, whether by accident or

---

[29] *Dark Interpreter: The Discourse of Romanticism* (Ithaca, NY: Cornell University Press, 1980), 245–7.

intentionally, it was placed in the 'Sibylline Leaves' section and not with the additional poems), it may, as Coburn suggests, have originated in two short Notebook fragments of 1807.[30] Two attempts at part of stanza IV exist on paper watermarked 1819 (but are dated 'much later' by E. H. Coleridge), and in a Notebook entry that Coburn dates *c*. September 1825 (*CN* iv. 5245) we find Coleridge making two attempts to work out a rhyme-scheme for stanza II:

<blockquote>

    For he dwelt at large,
As gay and innocent as the pretty shame
Of Babe, that rising to the menac'd charge,   aim
With wily shiness & with cheek aglow   large
From its twi-clustringed hiding-place of Snow   shame
Tempts & eludes   charge
                                  glow
                                  snow
                                  kiss
                                  miss
                   –cove?   targe
Of Babe, that from its hiding-place of Snow
Twy clustr'd, rising to the menac'd Charge
Tempts and eludes the happy Father's kiss
Which well may glance aside yet never miss
When the sweet Mark emboss'd so sweet a Targe

</blockquote>

The germ of the poem may have been in existence as early as 1807, and it may have been 'germinating a very long time', as Coburn remarks (*CN* ii. 3056 n); but the impulse that made Coleridge write the poem, refashioning some older material for a new context but creating most of the text anew, almost certainly derived from a meeting with Sara Hutchinson at Ramsgate in 1823.

On 14 October 1823 Sara Hutchinson wrote to her cousin Thomas Monkhouse

Coleridge who arrived on Saturday & called upon us yesterday—almost smothered her [the baby] with kisses which, tho' she endured them with patience, did not, her Mother observed, give her as much satisfaction as those of a younger Beau.[31]

The baby was Mary Monkhouse, daughter of Thomas and Jane Monkhouse, and the women were not alone in noticing how she 'endured' Coleridge's kisses. The poet made this episode the dramatic centre of

[30] *CN* ii. 3056, 3075 and nn.
[31] *The Letters of Sara Hutchinson*, ed. Kathleen Coburn (London: Routledge & Kegan Paul, 1954), p. xxxi, n., 264.

the poem that became 'The Pang More Sharp Than All'. At the same time he created for it devices typical of his later poetry: personification, allegory—the poem is subtitled 'An Allegory'—and 'faery' material. The result is no less anguished than earlier poems in Coleridge's 'confessional' mode, and it may be that because of its personal content it (unlike the more distanced 'Constancy to an Ideal Object') was not published in the collections of 1828 and 1829.

The poem begins with an unnamed personification, a Boy who is evidently Love, and who is troped to the 'faery' image of 'some Elfin Knight in kingly court', who, 'having won all guerdons in his sport, | Glides out of view'. This carefully controlled stanza of eight pentameter lines rhyming abbacddc has an element of pathos but does not prepare us for the chagrin of stanza II. Here the absent child is linked with 'the pretty shame | Of babe, that tempts and shuns the menaced kiss | From its twy-cluster'd hiding place of snow!' The compound adjective created for the mother's breasts—'twy-cluster'd' is a Coleridgean coinage[32]—is related to other double sources as in 'The Two Founts', and the image of mother and infant, usually one of Coleridge's most positive ones, is here transformed. A typical use would be in lines 14–16 of 'The Day-Dream', a poem explicitly addressed to Sara Hutchinson:

> I guess
> It would have made the loving mother dream
> That she was softly bending down to kiss
> Her babe . . .[33]

This sort of image can appear where one least expects it, as in *The Statesman's Manual*:

For never can I look and meditate on the vegetable creation without a feeling similar to that with which we gaze at a beautiful infant that has fed itself at its mother's bosom, and smiles in its strange dream of obscure yet happy sensations.[34]

But the poet's resentment is scarcely concealed in 'The Pang More Sharp Than All'. The babe and its mother are aspects of the same female, with the onlooking but unmentioned Sara Hutchinson making

---

[32] See James C. McCusick, ' "Living Words": Samuel Taylor Coleridge and the Genesis of the *OED*', *Modern Philology*, 90 (1992), 1–45, 43. McCusick also notes that 'warmthless' (1. 2) does not occur in English before this poem.

[33] *CPW* i. 387. 'The Day-Dream'—not to be confused with 'A Day-Dream'—was published in the *Morning Post* for 16 Oct. 1802 and not again in Coleridge's lifetime.

[34] *The Statesman's Manual, Lay Sermons*, 71.

a third—tempting and teasing with kiss and 'twy-cluster'd hiding-place of snow!' This image charged with chagrin leads to the bitter conclusion, 'Twice wretched he who hath been doubly blest!'

In keeping with the greater complexity of feeling in stanza II, the rhyme scheme is also more complex: ababccdebbed. In the 1825 Notebook entry previously mentioned, we find Coleridge trying to work out a rhyme scheme for this stanza, and the order of the last three rhymes of the second version there is that of the final version, though the wording of the lines is not the same. Certainly Coleridge devoted an unusual amount of workmanship both to the completion of this material and to the allegory. In stanza III the nameless boy is gone, but has been replaced by a sister and brother, Esteem and Kindness. Yet the poet remains devoted to the absent child, whose internalized image is evoked in memorable lines in stanza IV:

> For still there lives within my secret heart
> The magic image of the magic child . . .

This stanza is evidently a rewriting of manuscript material first printed by James Dykes Campbell in 1893 and then by E. H. Coleridge (*CPW* i. 457). In what appear to be two previous starts, the second (and longer) introduces 'Graveyard' imagery after the magic child has departed:

> A Blank my Heart, and Hope is dead and buried,
> Yet the deep yearning will not die; but Love
> Clings on and cloathes the marrowless remains,
> Like the fresh moss that grows on dead men's bones,
> Quaint mockery! and fills its scarlet cups
> With the chill dewdamps of the Charnel House.

This imagery, both melodramatic and inappropriate, was wisely omitted from the final version of the poem, just as years earlier Coleridge had eliminated the charnel-house imagery of 'The Rime of the Ancient Mariner' before publishing it in *Sibylline Leaves*. A tightly organized stanza, rhyming ababacbcbc, replaces the longer MS fragment (which breaks into rather limp blank verse after its fourth line), and this new stanza introduces 'faery' imagery derived from Spenser—Coleridge's own note refers the reader to Book III, canto ii, stanza 19 of *The Faerie Queene*—thus linking it with stanza I:

> The magic image of the magic Child,
> Which there he made up-grow by his strong art,
> As in that crystal orb—wise Merlin's feat,—
> The wondrous 'World of Glass', wherein inisled
> All long'd-for things their beings did repeat . . .

There is nevertheless a certain irony here. Merlin's 'world of glass' is a hollow mirror in which Britomart first sees her future love, Artegall. Though she suffers from the wound inflicted by 'Imperious Love', we know that consummation is in store; indeed, Britomart is given a vision of this in the next Canto. In Coleridge's poem the crystal orb retains an image of perpetual longing, and so the poet's state is one of continued deprivation—'To live and yearn and languish incomplete!'

In the fifth and last stanza the personifications of the third return to engage in a little drama in which Kindness puts on the 'faded robe' of the absent child, 'And inly shrinking from her own disguise | Enacts the faery Boy that's lost and gone.' The collapse of the personifications constituting the poet's inner world becomes the poem's very subject: the miming of the 'faery' world fails to establish a credible reality, and the poem's personifications fade into abstractions as the poet exclaims, 'O worse than all! O pang all pangs above | Is Kindness counterfeiting absent Love!' The note of acceptance sounded in 'Constancy to an Ideal Object' and in other late poems such as 'Duty Surviving Self-Love' (1826) and 'The Improvisatore' (1827) has at least temporarily given way, after the poet's encounter with the undesiring object of his desire, to a cry of anguish and of anger. To this extent, 'The Pang More Sharp Than All' resembles the two lyrics discussed at the beginning of this chapter. However, the richness of the poem's imagery, figuration, and rhetorical structures gives the poem a sense of objective being, barely containing the raw feelings that went into it, but nevertheless containing them so that they are accessible to the reader.

'Love's Apparition and Evanishment'

On 18 August 1833 Coleridge wrote to Charles Aders referring to 'a little poem I composed from a rude conception which I accidentally found in one of my old "Fly-catchers" (Flieger-fänger) or Mss Day Books for *impounding* (Einsperrung) Stray Thoughts, as I was lying in my bed, some three or four mornings ago, after my Gruel' (*CL* vi. 956). He enclosed a version of the poem 'in hopes you may read it to dear Mrs. Aders'. Then on 5 November he sent J. G. Lockhart a 'corrected copy' of the poem, saying, 'Henry N. Coleridge thought so highly of the grace and metrical movement of a little poem . . . that I am encouraged to inclose a corrected copy of it, for Mrs Lockhart, if she finds it legible' (*CL* vi. 972–3). Characteristically, Coleridge sends the poem not for the men but for their wives, assigns the praise of it to someone else, and revises it soon after writing it. In these ways, while conscious of the 'grace' of what he has produced, he takes evasive action against critical comparisons with his major poetry.

Actually, Coleridge had already revised the poem before sending it to Aders. He had sent a version to Thomas Pringle for publication in Pringle's annual *Friendship's Offering*, and then wrote to Pringle (letter endorsed 13 August 1833) offering to send 'a greatly improved copy of the poem', which he referred to as a '*Madrigal*', particularly with respect to 'the irregularity in the distances of the corresponding Rhymes, in that I gave you—as well as in the greater *perspicuity* in the Allegory' (*CL* vi. 952). Subsequently he wrote to Pringle again, complaining of the printer's failure to observe his instructions for capitals and small capitals, a point already discussed in the Introduction above. As we can see, the poet devoted an impressive amount of attention to this poem despite his attempt to appear diffident about it.

The poem, twenty-eight lines in length, was published in *Friendship's Offering* for 1834 (355–6), signed and dated August 1833. It was entitled 'Love's Ghost and Re-Evanition/ An Allegoric Romance'. Both title and subtitle demand comment. 'Evanition', according to the *OED*, is derived from 'evanish'—a much older word—on the model of 'abolition'; the first example is from Horace Walpole in 1797. When the poem was first collected in the *Poetical Works* of 1834, however, it was entitled 'Love's Apparition and Evanishment'. An older word had been preferred to a comparatively recent coinage. As for the subtitle, Coleridge had abandoned 'Madrigal' for 'Allegoric Romance' in *Friendship's Offering*. His original choice was doubtless an outgrowth of his interest in Italian madrigals, as expressed in a long Notebook entry of *c.* 1805 (*CN* ii. 2599 and n.). There Coleridge had written of the 16th-century madrigals of Giovanni Strozzi:

Of this exquisite Polish, of this perfection of *Art*, the following Madrigals are given as specimens, and as mementoes to myself, if ever I should be happy enough to resume poetic composition, to attempt a union of these—taking the whole of the latter, and as much of the former as is compatible with a poem's being perused with greater pleasure the second or the 20th time, than the first.

Nine of the madrigals here translated were later published in chapter 16 of the *Biographia Literaria*. Coleridge must have decided that the poem he had written was not very much like Strozzi's (which, among other things, typically comprise between eight and eleven lines), and he chose the far more appropriate subtitle 'An Allegoric Romance'.

The poem begins with one of Coleridge's almost obsessively

repeated thematic images: 'Like a lone Arab, old and blind'.[35] We have seen what a range of meanings the blind man had for Coleridge in Chapter 2. Like the blind man of the 'Limbo' constellation, the Arab of this poem 'Upturns his eyeless face from Heaven to gain [aid]'; and like the blind Arab of 'The Blossoming of the Solitary Date-Tree', he is presented explicitly as an analogue for Coleridge. Both in 'Love's Apparition' and the 'Date-Tree' his blindness is correlative to the absence of love, something that would have been further accentuated had Coleridge kept his original MS reading 'lorn Arab' (BL Add MS 34225 f 15; *CPW* ii. 1088). In this later poem,[36] his situation is a dangerous one: abandoned by his fellows, he is surrounded by poisonous serpents. The 'Dipsads' of *Friendship's Offering* were changed to 'sand-asps', obviating the need for the gloss 'The asps of the sand-deserts, anciently named', but also effacing the link that Coleridge had originally wanted to allude to the 'Dipsas' as one of the 'complicated monsters' of *Paradise Lost* (x. 523–6).[37] However, the 'corrected copy' that was sent to J. G. Lockhart reads 'Sand Asps', indicating that Coleridge changed his mind after *Friendship's Offering* had gone to press.[38]

With line 10, the seated figure becomes Coleridge himself, and his situation seems much as it was at the beginning of 'The Garden of Boccaccio':

> Even thus, in vacant mood, one sultry hour,
> Resting my eye upon a drooping plant,
> I sate upon the couch of camomile . . .

The 'couch of camomile' has an effect similar to that of the engraving after Stothard in 'The Garden of Boccaccio' in altering the poet's consciousness, but with very different results. Where the first brought Coleridge's imagination back to Italy, the world of courtly love, and 'faery', the couch of camomile stirs the ghost of his love for Sara Hutchinson for the last time, at least in poetry. The most prominent

[35] My text is the *Friendship's Offering* version, as the *Poetical Works* of 1834 does not follow Coleridge's careful instructions about capitalization and includes 'L'Envoy', which I do not think belongs with the poem (see below). However, I refer to the title by which the poem is generally known, and I note Coleridge's textual revisions.

[36] I agree with Tim Fulford that at least part of 'The Blossoming of the Solitary Date-Tree' belongs to the period *c.* 1802. See 'Paradise Rewritten? Coleridge's *The Blossoming of the Solitary Date-Tree*', *TWC* 24 (1993), 84.

[37] In the apparatus to the forthcoming *Poetical Works*, J. C. C. Mays notes that in the manuscript sent to Charles Aders Coleridge added 'See Par. Lost. Bk. X.'

[38] This MS, comprising variant versions of lines 4 and 7–17, is in the Cornell Wordsworth Collection (no. 2623), with a fragment of a letter to Lockhart postmarked 6 Nov. 1833. The letter (without the lines from 'Love's Apparition and Evanishment') appears in *CL* vi. 971–3).

association in poetry would be with lines 84–5 of the 'Letter to Sara Hutchinson': 'I would, that thou'dst be sitting all this while | Upon the sod-built Seat of Camomile—' (*Poems*, 352). In general the sod or turf seat had a special, shared meaning to members of the Wordsworth circle,[39] and George Whalley suggests persuasively that a real seat in the Gillmans' Highgate garden brought Coleridge memories of others associated with Sara Hutchinson, such as that commemorated in lines 13 and 14 of 'Inscription for a Fountain on a Heath'.[40]

The memories now brought to life are enlisted into a puppet-play of personifications, with the poet as the helpless spectator. As is also frequently the case in the edition of 1834, the small capitals that originally distinguished these personifications now disappear.[41] In an image prefigurative of Edgar Allan Poe, Hope is seen

> Drest as a bridesmaid, but all pale and cold,
> With roseless cheek, all pale and cold and dim (19–20)

The entrance of Love, 'a sylph in bridal trim', seems auspicious, but the effect of her kiss upon Hope is bitterly ironic:

> Alas! 'twas but a chilling breath
> Woke just enough of life in death
> To make Hope die anew.
> (26–8)

With another self-conscious gesture toward the world of his *Ancient Mariner*, Coleridge condemns both himself and the reader to be passive onlookers at the death of his own emotional life, a death imagined as occurring not once and for all but continuously.

---

[39] See Charles Bouslog, 'The Symbol of the Sod-Seat in Coleridge', *PMLA* 60 (1945), 802–10.

[40] Inscribed in *Sara's Poets* (no. 5) as 'Inscription on a jutting Stone, over a Spring.' See Whalley, *Coleridge and Sara Hutchinson* (London, 1955), 138.

[41] In addition to the revisions made in the letter to Lockhart, Coleridge made revisions on 2 sets of pages from *Friendship's Offering*, now in the PML. EHC, in an accompanying note, argues that these changes 'afford evidence that STC was at work on his poems in 1834, and more than helped to prepare that edition for the press'. *Friendship's Offering* was in print in the autumn of 1833, and not all of the changes that Coleridge made were incorporated in the 'deathbed edition'. For example, l. 11 was changed to 'With brow low-bent, within my garden bower' and l. 27 to 'Woke just enough of life in death'; the former change was not incorporated in 1834 while the latter was (from 'That woke enough of life in death'). Nevertheless, the direction of the changes in the Lockhart MS and in the Morgan revised pages is towards the 1834 text (although there is nothing in either to justify the abandonment of Coleridge's beloved small capitals).

'L' Envoy' and 'Desire'

The text of 'Love's Apparition and Evanishment' published in *Friendship's Offering* and, with some variants, in the *Poetical Works* of 1834 was twenty-eight lines long. However, some modern editions print four lines headed 'L'Envoy' at the end:

> In vain we supplicate the Powers above;
> There is no resurrection for the Love
> That, nursed in tenderest care, yet fades away
> In the chill'd heart by inward self-decay.
>
> $\qquad\qquad$ (*CPW* i. 489)

These lines appear, with minor variants, at the beginning of a draft manuscript of 'Love's Apparition and Evanishment', BL Add MS 34225 f 15:

> In vain I supplicate the Powers above
> There is no Resurrection for the Love
> That nurs'd with tenderest care yet fades away,
> In the chill'd heart by inward self-decay!

Another version of these lines was included in a letter Coleridge sent to his friend Thomas Allsop on 27 April 1824 (*CL* v. 360). However, Coleridge never published 'L'Envoy'. Confusion may have been caused inadvertently by Sara and Derwent Coleridge's 1852 *Poems of Samuel Taylor Coleridge*, where 'L'Envoy' is printed on the page immediately following 'Love's Apparition and Evanishment' (373, 374). However, these two texts are there presented as separate poems, and are listed as such in the Contents (xxvii). There is no textual authority for ending 'Love's Apparition and Evanishment' with 'L'Envoy', however closely the two may be linked thematically.

In the letter sent to Allsop, the poet makes it clear that the subject concerns 'kindness & kind attentions' now paid Coleridge by Anne Gillman (evidently in contrast to the recent past), remarking, 'I am content, well knowing that the genial glow of Friendship once deadened can never be rekindled' (*CL* v. 360). Two lines never published with 'L'Envoy' conclude the passage:

> Poor mimic of the past! the Love is o'er
> That must *resolve* to do what did itself of yore.[42]

The poem sent to Allsop originated in a Notebook passage dated 24 April 1824 (*CN* iv. 5146), to which Coleridge later added a note: 'n.b.

---

[42] These 2 lines were first published in *JDC* 644.

composed extempore, without taking my pen off the paper. Qy. Will they stand a second reading?' The Notebook verses certainly found a second reader, for, as in the case of 'Work without Hope', Anne Gillman also expressed her view: 'Mistaken'. Following this notation, on the next Notebook page, there occurs another textual outcropping: four more lines, which once more are related to what precedes them without becoming part of it. If we ignore Coleridge's deletions and follow his instructions to reverse the order of the third and fourth lines, these read:

> Desire, of pure Love born, itself's the same:
> A Pulse, that animates the outer frame,
> It but repeats the life-throb of the Heart—
> And takes the impress of the nobler part[.]

Another, weaker version of this quatrain, in which the organic imagery—'Pulse', 'animates', and 'life-throb',—is absent, appeared as 'Desire' in the *Poetical Works* of 1834.

The Notebook lines beginning 'Desire, of pure love born', were written, as Kathleen Coburn notes (*CN* iv. 5146 n.), below and opposite the excerpt from Sydney's *Arcadia* (*CN* iv. 4810) that Coleridge worked into 'First Advent of Love'. This juxtaposition suggests that Coleridge, returning to the beautiful lyric passage, wished to create by spatial juxtaposition a reminder of the two poles of love—its spires of myrtle wreath and its flashing sword. In his later poems about love, both aspects, as we have seen, are present, and a number of others as well; but the poetry of his last years increasingly emphasizes love's danger and its pain. His last poem on the subject, 'Love's Apparition and Evanishment', is a poem of the death of the heart, one that presents itself without the meliorations of friendship and wisdom—or even their very possibility. The death of Hope may remind us of the fictitiously dead Coleridge in 'To William Wordsworth', but her resurrection is a parody in which she dies anew. Her allegorical fate is in turn linked to the subject that occupied Coleridge most in the autumn of 1833: an epitaph fit for the occasion of his own anticipated death.

5 EPITAPHS

The last important poem to be written by Coleridge was printed under
the the simple title of 'Epitaph' as the final poem in the *Poetical Works*
of 1834. It is the culmination of a lifelong interest, for in the course of
his career Coleridge wrote numerous epitaphs and epitaph-like poems,
both for himself and for others. The earliest-published date from 1794[1]:
the 'Epitaph on an Infant'[2] that has already been mentioned in connection with the poet's conversation with William Rowan Hamilton, and
'Lines on a Friend Who Died of a Frenzy Fever Induced by Calum-
nious Reports' (*CPW* i. 76–8). These were included among 'Juvenile
Poems' in the *Poetical Works* of 1828, 1829, and 1834, while two epigrams in the form of mock-epitaphs written at Malta (*CN* ii. 2771 and
2779) were never published by the poet. However, Coleridge's two most
ambitious and most successful epitaphs were written during the period
of his later poetry. They are in some ways poems of different types, but
each of them has a special relation to Romantic inscription poetry.

In a celebrated essay, Geoffrey Hartman argues that the Romantic—
and after it the modern—lyric originated in epigrams and inscriptions,
and he discusses the close links between these modes and the epitaph.[3]
Hartman's initial example is Wordsworth's 'Lines left upon a Seat in a
Yew-tree', chosen as illustrating the 'convergence of elegiac and nature
poetry' and exhibiting the Romantic inscription poem's characteristic
'sense for a life (in nature) so hidden, retired, or anonymous that it is
perceived only with difficulty' (33). The poem published by Coleridge
in 1809 and later entitled 'A Tombless Epitaph' shares these characteristics at one remove: at one remove, because its title and closing lines
declare that it is inscribed 'here' instead of 'on monumental stone'—yet
these assertions serve to remind us of the poem's consanguinity with
epitaphs feigned to be inscribed in the natural world, as does its bringing into play the features of hidden path, forest shades, rill, glade, and

[1] The Greek epitaph that EHC prints and translates from the Estlin manuscript (*CPW* i. 68
n.) may well have been composed earlier.

[2] *CPW* i. 68; not to be confused with the beautiful and delicate 'Epitaph on an Infant',
beginning 'Its balmy lips the infant blest', of 1811 (*CPW* i. 417).

[3] 'Inscriptions and Romantic Nature Poetry', in *The Unremarkable Wordsworth* (Theory
and History of Literature ser. 34 (Minneapolis, Minn.: University of Minnesota Press, 1987),
31–46.

especially 'dark glen and secret dell' and 'long-neglected holy cave', constituting a hidden life in nature indeed. Coleridge's poem illustrates what Hartman terms 'the merging of epitaph and nature poetry' (34) as much as Wordsworth's does. It was, moreover, produced at a time when Wordsworth and Coleridge were closely associated in several projects centring on epitaphs.

'A Tombless Epitaph'

The autumn of 1809 and the winter of 1809–10 marked the last phase of the fruitful collaboration of Wordsworth and Coleridge, preceding their tragic personal rupture in October 1810. The subject was their shared interest in epitaphs, finding expression in Coleridge's 'A Tombless Epitaph', in Wordsworth's translations of Italian epitaphs by Gabriello Chiabrera (1522–1637), and in Wordsworth's three *Essays Upon Epitaphs*. The vehicle for some of this material was Coleridge's *Friend*, in which first appeared Coleridge's poem with its accompanying essay,[4] six of Wordsworth's translations of Chiabrera[5] and most of the first of the *Essays Upon Epitaphs*.[6] Behind these publications one senses an ongoing discussion of the nature of epitaphs. As in the golden period of 1797–8, it is at times hard to tell where one poet's contribution leaves off and the other's begins. Wordsworth used as some of his examples graveyard epitaphs that Coleridge had copied into his Notebooks while both were staying at Coleorton in the memorable winter of 1806–7[7]; some of Wordsworth's remarks on the *Essays Upon Epitaphs* seem to be drawn from Coleridge in practice; and it is impossible to say who introduced the other to Chiabrera.[8] Furthermore, it could be said that 'A Tombless Epitaph' takes up from 'To William Wordsworth', as the figure mourned is an aspect of Coleridge himself.

Satyrane, the idealized self who is the subject of 'A Tombless Epitaph', was the putative author of letters written by Coleridge from

[4] 2 (23 November 1809), 184–5.

[5] Wordsworth translated 9 epitaphs by Chiabrera. Six of these were published in *The Friend*: 28 Dec. 1809 (IV and VI); 4 Jan. 1810 (VIII and IX); and 22 Feb. 1810 (II and III). See *Poetical Works*, ed. E. de Selincourt (Oxford: Clarendon Press, 1947), iv. 248–53.

[6] *Friend*, 2 (22 Feb. 1810), 334–46. My citations of *Essays* 2 and 3 are from Wordsworth's *Prose Works*, while those from *Essay* 1 refer to *The Friend*.

[7] See e.g. epitaphs quoted in the third *Essay* (*Prose Works* ii. 92) and those from Coleridge's Notebooks printed as *CN* ii. 2982.

[8] Those tempted to assume Coleridge's priority in such matters should remember Wordsworth's proficiency in Italian literature while at Cambridge and afterwards.

Germany and published first in *The Friend* and then in the *Biographia*.[9] His is the figure in which Wallace Stevens found 'a persistent euphony . . . dressed in black, with large shoes and black worsted stockings, dancing on the deck of the Hamburg packet'.[10] This choice of alter ego is interesting, for Satyrane is not one of the most powerful knights of *The Faerie Queene*. 'A Satyres son yborn in forrests wylde' (I, vi. 21), he appears in Books I, III, and IV, helping heroines to the extent of his capacity, which is limited by his entirely earthly nature, as his name and lineage imply. Representing a purely natural goodness,[11] he is a self-consciously modest choice for Coleridge, but one that at the same time may express some serious inner conflicts.

Anything but modest is the prose that connects the untitled poem with the first letter. The name, Coleridge informs us, is that which he went by among his friends and familiars, 'SATYRANE, the Idoloclast, or breaker of Idols' (*Friend* ii. 185). This use of 'Idoloclast' antedates the first *OED* example by more than twenty years,[12] and Coleridge's use of it desynonymizes it from 'iconoclast', which the *OED* gives as identical in meaning. The breaker of idols destroys things that have been invested with value in themselves; Coleridge recognized that icons could represent the value of something else. Satryrane is represented as one joyous by nature who has devoted his life to opposing the idols of his age until, forced to recognize their power among his contemporaries, he withdraws into a bitter isolation.

When he was at length compelled to see and acknowledge the true state of the morals and intellect of his contemporaries, his disappointment was severe, and his mind, always thoughtful, became pensive and almost gloomy: for to love and sympathize with mankind was a necessity of his nature. Hence, as if he sought a refuge from his own sensibility, he attached himself to the most abstruse researches, and seemed to derive his purest delight from subjects that exercised the strength and subtlety of his understanding without awakening the feelings of his heart.[13]

[9] The original of the first of the 3 letters was written to Sara Fricker Coleridge on 3 Oct. 1798. It appeared in revised form, following the poem and the prose preface in *The Friend*, 2, for 23 Nov. 1809 (187–96).

[10] 'The Figure of the Youth As a Virile Poet', in *The Necessary Angel: Essays on Reality and the Imagination* (London: Faber & Faber, 1951), 41.

[11] See Ronald A. Horton, 'Satyrane', *The Spenser Cyclopedia*, ed. A. C. Hamilton (Toronto: University of Toronto Press 1990), 628.

[12] His first use of the word comes even earlier, in a Notebook entry of Dec. 1803, beginning 'Motto for my Idoloclastes' and followed by a quotation from Locke (*CN* i. 1729).

[13] *Friend*, 2 (23 Nov. 1809), 187. Rooke appositely notes the similarity of phrasing to Coleridge's description of his 'Despondency' in a letter to Lady Beaumont dated 15 Apr. 1810 (*CL* iii. 287).

The prose portrait is thus a version of the 'metaphysical explanation' with the variant of Satyrane's becoming a figure of opposition.

Coleridge knew that he could hardly expect his reader to accept this fictitious identity at face value, the less so the better the reader knew him. 'You will grin,' he wrote to Southey in early November 1809, 'at my *modest* account of Satyrane, the Idoloclast, in no. 14—but what can I do?—I must wear a mask—' (*CL* iii. 261). At the same time he felt not only that the mask was essential to his purpose but also that it displayed a true aspect of himself. Annotating a copy of the 1812 reissue of *The Friend*, he wrote, 'I have always in the *better* parts of my character the Satyrane Idoloclastes.'[14] The poem celebrates these 'better parts', the joy that characterized Satyrane when he was young; but it differs from the prose account of his decline, showing once more the instability of Coleridge's self-explanations. Here it is 'Sickness' that:

> Whole years of weary days, besieg'd him close
> Even to the gates and outlets of his Life![15]

Nevertheless, he pursued his course as a poet, and in a delightful passage his exploration of the landscape of poetry is invoked:

> For not a hidden path, that to the shades
> Of the belov'd Parnassian forests leads,
> Lurk'd undiscover'd by him; not a rill
> There issues from the font of Hippocrene,
> But he had trac'd it onward to its' source
> Thro' open glade, dark glen, and secret dell,
> Knew the gay wild-flowers on its' banks, and cull'd
> Its' med'cinable herbs.

This is recognizably a version of the landscape of 'Kubla Khan', with its forests ancient as the hills, sacred river, and underground source. Coleridge would 'stroll' through such a scene as an alienated being in 'Work without Hope'; but in this poem of 1809 the portrait is of an enabled poet, one to whom the natural world reveals its mysteries. There is even a touch here of Caliban's showing Prospero 'all the qualities o' th' isle, | The fresh springs, brine-pits, barren place and fertile', in *The*

---

[14] See Jonathan Wordsworth, 'Some Unpublished Coleridge Marginalia', *The Times Literary Supplement*, 58 (14 June 1957), 369. Coleridge's note appears beside the letter from 'Mathetes' (John Wilson and Alexander Blair) originally publ. in *The Friend*, 14 Dec. 1809.

[15] ll. 15–16. I follow the *Friend* version here. This text is, with the exception of incidentals and its lack of a title, identical with later ones with the exception of l. 36, where 'full of light and love!' becomes 'full of Life and Love!' from *Sibylline Leaves* onward.

Tempest[16]—a resonance that would be in keeping with one aspect of Satyrane's identity. Yet philosophic wisdom is here seen as belonging to him as well, for Satyrane can also be identified with Prospero:

> Yea, oft alone
> Piercing the long-neglected holy cave,
> The haunt obscure of old Philosophy,
> He bade with lifted torch its' starry walls
> Sparkle, as erst they sparkled to the flame
> Of od'rous lamps tended by Saint and Sage.

This is the poet as magus, with a distinct echo of Alexander Pope's famous description of his grotto:

And when you have a mind to light it up, it affords you a very different Scene: it is finished with Shells interspersed with Pieces of Looking-glass in angular forms; and in the Ceiling is a Star of the same material, at which when a Lamp (of orbicular figure of thin Alabaster) is hung in the Middle, a thousand pointed Rays glitter and are reflected over the Place.[17]

In both passages there is, of course, the suggestion of the activation of the poetic imagination. The protagonist of Coleridge's poem, far from being disabled by his philosophical speculations, is able to incorporate them into his poetic being, very much as Coleridge had once hoped to do.

In a note to the poem published in *The Friend*, Coleridge wrote, 'Imitated, though in the movements rather than the thoughts, from the VIIth of Gli Epitafi of *Chiabrera*' (*Friend* ii. 184 n.). We can see what Coleridge means from the very beginning of 'A Tombless Epitaph'. Chiabrera's epitaphs generally begin with the naming of the subject and what was most notable about him, and Coleridge does this with a difference:

> 'Tis true, IDOLOCLASTES SATYRANE
> (So call him, for so mingling blame with praise
> And smiles with anxious looks, his earliest friends,
> Masking his birth-name, wont to character
> His wild-wood fancy and impetuous zeal)

---

[16] I. ii. 339–40. Kathleen Coburn suggests another echo, of *The Prelude*, i. 35–8, a passage that she notes Coleridge wrote out (with variants) in a Notebook in May 1804 (*CN* ii. 2086, f 40 and n.). Cf. especially Wordsworth's 'To drink wild water, and to pluck green herbs, | And gather fruits fresh from their native bough.'

[17] Quoted by Morris R. Brownell, *Alexander Pope & the Arts of Georgian England* (Oxford: Clarendon Press, 1978), 255.

Chiabrera's epitaph begins, in Wordsworth's translation:

> True is it that Ambrosio Salinero
> With an untoward fate was long involved
> In odious litigation; and full long,
> Fate harder still! had he to endure assaults
> Of racking malady.[18]

Coleridge transposes Chiabrera's literal details onto a figurative plane, except for the matter of illness, which will appear later. The parts of Chiabrera's poem most like Coleridge's are lines 9 to 13:

> Not a covert path
> Leads to the dear Parnassian forest's shade,
> That might from him be hidden; not a track
> Mounts to the pellucid Hippocrene, but he
> Had traced its windings.

The rest is pure Coleridge; and as he remarks in his note, it is 'the movements rather than the thoughts' of Chiabrera's verse that he has tried to capture—a comparatively slow, reflective turning from one major aspect of the subject to another, with the transitions often occurring in mid-line and the conclusion slightly muted. Coburn rightly calls it 'a most ingenious improvisation on a theme, with only a few lines of the original surviving'.[19]

* * *

During the later years of his life Coleridge's thoughts became further occupied with epitaphs, culminating in the completion of his own. We can see this interest expressed in a number of other epitaphs and epitaph-like poems, some serious and some, like the 'Epitaph of the Present Year in the monument of Thomas Fuller' (*CPW* ii. 975), witty. Necessarily of special interest are those epitaphs that refer to the poet himself, such as the 'Epitaphium Testamentarium' in Latin and Greek that once formed part of 'Lines Suggested by the Last Words of Berengarius':

The Epitaph of S. T. C., written by himself at the point of death. The things I shall leave are either nothing or of no value, or scarce my own. The dregs I give to death: I restore the rest, O Christ! to thee.[20]

---

[18] *Poetical Works*, ed. E. de Selincourt (Oxford, 1947), iv. 250–1. Numbered v by Wordsworth, this translation did not appear in *The Friend*, and was first published in 1837.

[19] *CN* ii. (Notes), App. A: 'Coleridge's Knowledge of Italian', 403.

[20] Transl. by John Beer, *Poems*, 467 n. The '*Epitaphium Testamentarium*', as noted in Ch. 3, was reduced to a footnote when 'Lines Suggested by the Last Words of Berengarius' appeared

This heartfelt exclamation prefigures the 'Epitaph' of 1833. At the other end of the spectrum are grotesque or comic epigraphs, such as the one Coleridge sent to Frederic M. Reynolds on 25 August 1828 as if recently composed, although it actually dates back (with minor variants) to 12 September 1803.[21] The subject is nightmares of death that the poet had in Edinburgh, resulting in screams that woke the house:

> Here lies poor Col at length, and without Screaming
> Who died as he had always lived, *a dreaming*—
> Shot with a Pistol by the Gout within,
> Alone and all unknown, at Embro' in an Inn.

Two of Coleridge's accompanying remarks are of great interest. He writes that he composed the poem in a dream, the same kind of origin he had claimed for 'Kubla Khan'; and he makes an unusual reference to the death of his father: 'and some night or other I shall probably die as my father did'. The Rev. John Coleridge had died unexpectedly when Samuel was in his ninth year, and the poet seldom mentions this traumatic event. The facts that he brings this up the day after having been '*hook'd*' on to the whirlabout Car of the Portly God, Bacchus' (*CL* vi. 754) at a party given by Reynolds, and that he fictionalizes the epitaph as recently written in a dream, suggest that Coleridge was trying to cope with anxieties about death by indulging in grotesque humour. To this same category belong two mock epitaphs that he sent to Eliza Aders in the letter of November 1833 [?] that also included one of the versions of the epitaph he wrote in earnest. First he pretended to make an epitaph for himself out of a line from Ovid: 'Non formosus erat, sed erat facundus Ulysses.' This becomes:

> S. T. Coleridge Ætat. suae 63.
> Not/ handsome/ was/ but was/ eloquent [.]

Coleridge says he sends it to accompany the gift of a portrait engraving of himself after Abraham Wivell (see Supplementary Note, below) and that he has written these lines under one of the other proofs.[22] He then recasts the idea in English verse:

in the *Literary Souvenir* for 1827, and disappeared altogether from the *Poetical Works* of 1828, 1829, and 1834. Nevertheless, it obviously had deep personal meaning for Coleridge, and its use of Greek words anticipates some versions of the later 'Epitaph'.

[21] *CL* vi. 754; *CPW* ii. 970; *CL* ii. 992 n. Coleridge also recalled this epitaph in a Notebook entry of 1826 (*CN* v. 5360 and n.).

[22] *CL*: vi. 969. That proof had been sent to Henry Nelson Coleridge. See Supplementary Note: 'The Abraham Wivell Portrait'.

Translation
> 'In truth, he's no beauty!' cried Moll, Poll, and Tab,
> But they all of them own'd he'd the gift of the Gab.

This is followed, in an astonishing shift of mood, by a postscript including version 5 (see below) of an epitaph he had written for himself in earnest. Before we discuss that poem in the course of its evolution, it is appropriate to consider another very late poem which, while not itself an epitaph, displays epitaph-like qualities.

'*My Baptismal Birth-Day*'

Although Henry Nelson Coleridge thought 'My Baptismal Birth-day' was Coleridge's last poem,[23] it existed in some form in August 1833, before all but the first version of the 'Epitaph' itself. In recounting his visit to Coleridge at Highgate on 5 August 1833, Ralph Waldo Emerson wrote:

When I rose to go, he said, 'I do not know whether you care about poetry, but I will repeat some verses I lately made on my baptismal anniversary,' and he recited with strong emphasis, standing, ten or twelve lines, beginning, 'Born unto God in Christ—'[24]

On 6 August Coleridge sent the poem to Thomas Pringle for publication in *Friendship's Offering*, remarking that it had been written 'on my spiritual Birth-day, October 28' (*CL* vi. 950–1). If that was indeed the case, 'My Baptismal Birth-day' must have been composed no later than 1832, and not in 1833 as generally believed;[25] or perhaps Coleridge meant that the conception for such a poem came to him at the earlier date. As a declaration of faith, it is closely related to the 'Epitaph', but in its stridency it differs in tone from most of Coleridge's other poems on spiritual subjects.

In form 'My Baptismal Birth-day' is, like 'Work without Hope', an unconventionally structured sonnet, rhyming, in this instance, ababccddcfefss. The juxtaposition of spiritual life and the anticipation of physical death is emphasized in *Friendship's Offering* by the sub-title 'LINES COMPOSED ON A SICK BED, UNDER SEVERE BODILY SUFFERING,

---

[23] See *Coleridge: The Critical Heritage*, 651 (from the *Quarterly Review* for Aug. 1834).

[24] This is of course the beginning of 'My Baptismal Birth-day', which is 14 lines long in its published version. See Emerson, *English Traits* (London, 1856), 6–7.

[25] See e.g. *CPW* i. 491. Coleridge was born on 21 Oct. 1772 and presumably baptized later that month.

ON MY SPIRITUAL BIRTHDAY, OCTOBER 28th'.[26] The antithetical structure and its final resolution are also more clearly indicated in *Friendship's Offering* by spaces after lines 6 and 12.[27] The way in which this contrast was elaborated may, as James Dykes Campbell first suggested,[28] owe something to Sir Thomas Browne:

Every man hath a double Horoscope, one of his humanity, his birth; another of his Christianity, his baptisme, and from this doe I compute or calculate my Nativity, not reckoning those *Horae combustae* and odde dayes, or esteeming my selfe any thing, before I was my Saviours, and inrolled in the Register of Christ: Whosoever enjoyes not this life, I count him but an apparition, though he weare about him the sensible affections of flesh. In these morall acceptations, the way to be immortal is to die dayly; nor can I think I have the true theory of death, when I contemplate a skull, or behold a Skeleton with those vulgar imaginations it casts upon us; I have therefore inlarged that common *Memento mori*, into a more Christian memorandum, *Memento quatuor Novissima*, those four inevitable points of us all, Death, Judgement, Heaven, and Hell.[29]

In the course of developing an essential contrast between the forces of nature and those of the spirit, Coleridge makes, as we have seen in a number of other late poems, a reference to one of his earlier works—'France: An Ode' (1798). In the climactic lines of that poem, he presents himself as a prophet of Nature:

> Yes, while I stood and gazed, my temples bare,
> And shot my being through earth, sea, and air,
> Possessing all things with intensest love,
> O Liberty! my spirit felt thee there.

In 'My Baptismal Birth-day' the relationship between poet and nature is, in contrast, adversarial: 'Let then earth, sea, and sky | Make war against me!'[30] The elements that the poet had seen as uniting with him in an affirmation of freedom are now represented as the enemies of the Christian at war with the natural world.

---

[26] *Friendship's Offering* for 1834, 163. In the ms the main title is preceded by the same statement, with slightly different wording.

[27] In addition to dispensing with these, the *Poetical Works* of 1834 eliminated Coleridge's small capitals and, in 3 instances, his italics. Nevertheless, I cite this text here because it incorporates changes beyond any that H. N. Coleridge can be assumed to have made on his own editorial authority.

[28] *JDC* 645.   [29] *Religio Medici* (4th edn., London, 1656), 95–6.

[30] *CPW* i. 247, ll. 102–5; i. 491, ll. 9–10. Whether by intention or not, these lines also contrast with part of Wordsworth's sonnet 'To Toussaint L'Ouverture': 'Thou hast left behind | Powers that will work for thee; air, earth, and skies;' *Poems in Two Volumes*, ed. Jared Curtis (Ithaca, NY, 1983), 161.

From its beginning, 'My Baptismal Birth-day' displays a spiritual aggressiveness generally uncharacteristic of Coleridge, and even 'God's child in Christ adopted' is toned down from the 'Born unto God in CHRIST' of *Friendship's Offering*. In lines 3 to 4, the change from the plural 'we call' of *Friendship's Offering* to the singular emphasizes the intensely personal nature of the poet's belief in 'that name, by which I call | The Holy One, the Almighty God, my Father'. Coleridge goes so far as to declare himself one of the Elect: the 'mighty master's seal' of line 11 alludes to Rev. 7: 3, where the voice of an angel cries, 'Hurt not the earth, neither the sea, nor the trees, till we have sealed the servants of our God in their foreheads.' This allusion would have been even clearer in the manuscript Coleridge sent Pringle, where the reading is 'on my front I shew'. Perhaps the revision was made because 'front' is literary, an archaic word for 'forehead', while 'heart' is in keeping with the language of intense feeling that pervades the poem.

Although Coleridge had by 1832 ceased to be an admirer of Edward Irving, 'My Baptismal Birth-day' allows us a glimpse of the part of the poet which once responded to that chiliastic preacher. The poem is characterized, as James D. Boulger remarks, by 'somewhat hysterical straining',[31] though perhaps it is not so much a statement of 'the extreme Calvinist position', as Boulger puts it, as a series of personal ejaculations about the after-life by a man feeling the approach of death and trying to reassure himself of salvation. The forcing of the rhetoric concludes with a clumsy borrowing from the famous last lines of Donne's tenth *Divine Meditation* ('Death, be not proud'):

> Is that a death-bed where a Christian lies?—
> Yes! but not his—'tis Death there dies.
>
> One short sleepe past, we wake eternally,
> And death shall be no more; death, thou shalt die.[32]

Coleridge must have recognized that any comparison would be to his disadvantage. His own final spiritual statement would be very different.

'Epitaph'

The first rendition of Coleridge's true 'Epitaph' probably comprised four lines supposedly written in 1807 in a copy of the *Todten Tanz*:

---

[31] *The Calvinist Temper in English Poetry* (The Hague, 1981), 373.
[32] *The Poems of John Donne*, ed. Herbert J. C. Grierson (2 vols., London: Oxford University Press, 1963 [1912]), i. 326.

ESTEESEE'S αυτοεπιταφιον

Here lies a Poet—or what once was He.
Pray, gentle Reader, pray for S. T. C.,
That he who threescore years, with toilsome breath,
Found death in life, may now find life in death.[33]

The tone of this short poem is both humble and intimate. The first word of the title introduces a transliteration of Coleridge's initials with the confidence that the reader will recognize their applicability. The fourth line expresses a fundamental Christian paradox (*cf.* John 12: 25: 'He that loveth his life shall lose it; and he that hateth his life in this world shall keep it unto life eternal') and at the same time recalls one of the most dramatic situations in *The Rime of the Ancient Mariner*—the game of dice in which Life-in-Death wins the Ancient Mariner from Death.[34] These two elements—the existence of the author/subject on a plane of reality signified by his initials, and the allusion to his past accomplishment as a poet—would be featured in all versions of the 'Epitaph'.

A sense of increasing urgency about his 'Epitaph' manifests itself in Coleridge during the autumn of 1833. From 26 or 27 October to 5 November—a period of ten or eleven days—he produced no fewer than six versions of the poem.[35] Versions 2 and 3 were written on the endpapers of Nehemiah Grew's *Cosmologia Sacra* (1711, copy in BL). The first, entitled 'ETESIS's [*sic*] Epitaph' first read:

Here lies a Poet: or what once was He!
Pause Traveller pause and pray for S. T. C.
That He who many a year with toil of Breath
Found Death in Life, may here find Life in Death.

[33] Published (from an untraced original) by Mrs Henry Sandford, *Thomas Poole and His Friends* (2 vols., London, 1888), ii. 301. There are problems concerning this text and its dating. As printed by Mrs Sandford, it goes on with two lines that correspond to lines 7–8 of the final 'Epitaph': 'Mercy for praise, *to be forgiven* for fame, | He asked, and hop'd, thro' Christ. Do thou the same.' Modern editors consider that these two lines were added by Mrs Poole after the publication of the *Poetical Works* of 1834: see *JDC* 646 and Whalley in *CM* ii. 904 n. However, a problem still exists in that the form in which the text is given by Mrs Sandford is closer to versions 4 and 5 (both in letters; see below) than to the 1834 edn., particularly in that 'to be forgiven' is not italicized in the latter while it is underlined in versions 4 and 5, and Mrs Sandford pointedly comments 'There is something that goes to the heart in the sight of those three words "to be forgiven", underlined by Coleridge's own hand.' It is, furthermore, puzzling that Coleridge specifies 'threescore years' when he was 35 in 1807.

[34] 'The Nightmare LIFE-IN-DEATH' was not so named until the version of the poem published in *Sibylline Leaves* in 1817. However, as indicated in the preceding note, there are problems about the date of Mrs Sandford's version.

[35] See Whalley in *CM* ii. 903–4n.

To this base, Coleridge added a new first line—'Stop, Christian Visitor! stop, child of God,' inserted an 'O' before 'Pause', and added a new second line with directions for its insertion:

> And read with gentle heart! Beneath this sod
> There lies a Poet & c.

Below, he wrote a prose sentence further emphasizing the importance of his initials: 'Inscription on the tombstone of one not unknown; yet more commonly known by the Initials of his Name, than by the Name itself.'

This new poem—for such it really is—begins with an adaptation of a classical thematic statement, the *Siste Viator* that was frequently a feature of Greek and Latin epigraphs, incorporating with it the classical convention that it is the deceased who addresses the traveller.[36] Here there is also a link with the first *Essay on Epitaphs*, where Wordsworth had written of 'the Traveller, leaning upon one of the Tombs, or reposing in the coolness of it's shade, whether he had halted from weariness or in compliance to the invitation, "Pause, Traveller!" so often found upon the Monuments'.[37] Wordsworth had himself used the formula at the beginning of 'Lines left upon a Seat in a Yew-tree': '—Nay, Traveller! rest.'[38] Yet Coleridge was dissatisfied both with 'Visitor', so evidently a ghost of *Viator*, and with the abrupt closure. He turned forward one leaf and began again, this time with a title referring to his expected burial place:

Epitaph

in Hornsey Church yard

Hic Jacet S. T. C.

> Stop, Christian Passer-by! Stop, Child of God!
> And read with gentle heart. Beneath this sod
> There lies a Poet: or what once was He.
> O
> ~~Up~~lift thy soul in prayer for S. T. C.
> That he who many a year with toil of breath
> Found death in life may here find life in death.
> Mercy for praise, to be forgiven for fame
> He ask'd, and hoped thro' Christ. Do thou the same.

Version 3 eliminates the repeated 'pause' of 2 and substitutes, as revised, the vocative injunction 'O lift thy soul in prayer.' Two new

---

[36] On these elements in the classical epitaph, see Richard Lattimore, *Themes in Greek and Latin Epigraphs* (Urbana, Ill.: University of Chicago Press, 1962), 230–4.

[37] *Friend*, 2 (22 Feb. 1810), 339.   [38] *Lyrical Ballads 1798*, 35.

closing lines bring the poem to its final length. These are glossed by
Coleridge in a note to version 7, sent in a letter to J. G. Lockhart dated
5 November 1833 (*CL* vi. 973). There the poet explains that 'for' in line
7 has the force of 'instead of'. This expression has a Latin base, illustrated in an earlier Notebook entry, in which Coleridge writes
'However, for myself—veniam pro laude peto' [I seek mercy instead of
praise].[39] Line 7 may therefore be paraphrased: '[He asked for] mercy
instead of praise, to be forgiven instead of fame.' The humility of this
statement accords much more with Coleridge's typical religious attitude than does the bravado of 'My Baptismal Birth-day'. With its new
ending, the poem also meets the desiderata stated in Wordsworth's first
Essay on Epitaphs:

It ought to contain some Thought or Feeling belonging to the mortal or immortal part of our Nature touchingly expressed; and if that be done, however
general or even trite the sentiment may be, every man of pure mind will read
the words with pleasure and gratitude.[40]

Coleridge's 'Epitaph' was now basically in its final form; a few changes,
the most important of which involved the introduction of Greek and
Latin words, were yet to be made, although no words other than
English would appear in the final, printed text.

On 28 October 1833, only a day or two after writing the Grew versions, Coleridge wrote to J. H. Green, 'I send you the Epitaph, that I
rewrote last night, or rather re-*thought* (for I am now first to re-*write* it)'
(*CL* vi. 963). He continued with the statement about his initials already
made in version 2, and added the further element of Greek and Latin
words punning on them. The text itself differs from its immediate pre-
decessor in only four circumstances apart from incidentals. The poem
is now headed 'On a Tombstone'; the beginning of line 3 has been
inverted to read 'A Poet lies'; line 4 now begins 'O lift thy soul in prayer',
and 'to be forgiven' is underlined. Even fewer changes appear in what is
assumed to be the fifth version (see Supplementary Note), which was
sent to Eliza Aders in a letter conjecturally dated November 1833 (*CL*
vi. 969–70). Here the title is simply 'S. T. C.,' but it is preceded by the
statement:

The lines when printed would probably have on the preceding page this
advertisement

Epitaph on a Poet little known, yet better known by his [the] Initials of his
Name than by the Name itself.

[39] *CN* iii. 4121. In her note Coburn calls attention to this link with the 'Epitaph'. See also
Whalley in *CM* ii. 906 n.   [40] *Friend* 2: 341.

In line 3, 'was' has been replaced by the more modest 'seemed'; and for the first time since version 1 'toilsome breath' appears in line 5 instead of 'toil of breath'. Only the first of these changes would be retained.[41]

Version 6 of the 'Epitaph' is written on the inside back cover of Coleridge's Notebook 52 (BL Add Mss 47, 547). Here we see the poet struggling with other changes of wording. In line 2, he first wrote 'thy' but scored it out and wrote 'one' above it, making the reading conform with versions 4 and 5. 'Toil of breath' returns in line 5, and 'to be forgiven' is not underlined. At the end, the poet inscribed two queries. 'And read with gentle thought' is considered as a possible substitute in line 2, as is 'o lift thy heart' in line 4. At least part of Coleridge's motive here was probably to include the word 'heart' but not use it twice. It is in this manuscript, too, that Greek inscriptions, the significance of which will be discussed shortly, enter the text itself. Such inscriptions also appear more elaborately in what is considered the last manuscript version, sent in a letter to John Gibson Lockhart on 5 November 1833 (*CL* vi. 973); but the English text differs from that of version 7 only in incidentals. Finally, the *Poetical Works* of 1834, which contains no classical language, introduces one important change in line 2: 'breast' is substituted for 'heart'. As we have seen, Coleridge considered using 'gentle thoughts' in version 6, but there he also considered 'o lift thy heart' for line 4. 'Heart' now disappears from the poem completely, and with it any possible association with the 'gentle heart' of 'First Advent of Love'.[42] This completes Coleridge's revision of his 'Epitaph', though the manuscript versions, especially 6 and 7, retain interest and authority in their own right.

In the letter to Eliza Aders that included version 5, Coleridge made clear the qualities he wanted his epitaph to display, and in so doing linked the poem with 'A Tombless Epitaph'. Mrs Aders had sent him a vignette for a tombstone drawn by Maria Denman, evidently showing

[41] There may, however, have been a space between ll. 4 and 5, dividing the poem into 2 parts. So it is printed from the MS of the letter to Eliza Aders once in the possession of Arthur Duke Coleridge; see *Reminiscences* of Arthur Duke Coleridge, ed. J. A. Fuller-Maitland (London: Constable 1921), 44. The original letter is untraced and the text in *CL* is printed from a transcript (*CL* vi. 968 n.).

[42] Henry Nelson Coleridge's MS transcription of the 'Epitaph' (*TT* i. 450) differs from the 1834 text in some incidentals, but not in wording. A version published later in 1834, in a footnote to the *Quarterly*'s long review of the *Poetical Works*, 52 (Aug. and Nov. 1834), 292 n., begins line 4 with 'O, lift a thought'. The fact that the review has been ascribed to Henry Nelson Coleridge, e.g. Jackson (ed.), *Coleridge: The Critical Heritage* (London, 1971), 620, might lend this change some textual authority, but as the note is clearly an editorial addition made after the poet's death on 25 July 1834, the weak 'a thought' is likely to have been a scribal error or a misprint.

a Muse playing a musical instrument and wearing or displaying a laurel wreath.[43] Gracefully but firmly, Coleridge declined the offered design:

The homely, plain *church yard* Christian Verses would not be in keeping with a Muse (tho' a lovelier I never wooed), nor with a Lyre or Harp, or Laurel, or aught else *Parnassian* or allegorical. A rude old Yew-Tree or a mountain Ash with a grave or two or any other characteristics of a Village rude Church-yard—such a hint of Landscape was all, I meant, but if any figure rather that of an elderly man

> Thoughtful, with quiet tears upon his cheek.
> (*Tombless Epitaph*—see Sibylline Leaves)

Coleridge's connecting his 'Epitaph' with the earlier poem points up the interesting paradox of his position. He desires an epitaph without artifice—'plain *church yard* Christian Verses' of the sort he had taken down in Notebook entries from real gravestones. Nevertheless, the poem that he actually wrote, while displaying admirable simplicty of diction—the last line, for example, is virtually monosyllabic—could never be mistaken for one of those. Prosodically sophisticated in its use of enjambement (lines 2–3 and 7–8) and in its placing of full-breath pauses (in the middle of lines 1, 2, 7, and 8), self-allusive in line 6, and Latinate in structure in line 7, it uses the churchyard epitaph only as a point of departure. A classical allegory illustrating the poem would indeed have been inappropriate; for similar reasons Wordsworth critic-izes Chiabrera's personification of the 'sympathizing stream Sebeto in his epitaph for Lelius'.[44] However, the alternative iconic representa-tion that Coleridge is willing to envisage, one featuring 'a rude old Yew tree' as if out of Wordsworth's 'Lines left upon a Seat in a Yew-tree', with Coleridge himself, as the author of 'A Tombless Epitaph' some twenty-five years older, gives tacit recognition to the necessity for artifice.

In his letter to Eliza Aders, Coleridge introduced version 5 with the sketch of a tombstone bearing his own initials, remarking '*I* like this tomb stone very much' (*CL* vi. 969). This emphasizes the affinity of the poem with inscriptions, although it does not mean that the poet wished the 'Epitaph' to be engraved on his actual tombstone.[45] Rather, as E. H. Coleridge suggests, he probably wished an outline engraving in the shape of a tombstone to surround the text, 'and that this should

[43] *CL* vi. 969–70. The design is untraced, as is the original letter.
[44] *Essay on Epitaphs* III, in *The Prose Works of William Wordsworth*, ed. W. J. B. Owen and Jane Worthington Smyser (3 vols., Oxford, 1974), ii. 90. Wordsworth translated this epitaph twice; his wording in the *Essay* differs from that in the translation published as Epitaph VII in 1837.   [45] It was inscribed nearby in 1961; see Griggs, *CL* vi. 997.

illustrate, by way of a vignette, the last page of the volume'.[46] If such was his wish, it was not carried out, for the 'Epitaph' appears in 1834 with no vignette, although it appropriately closes the last volume, with the date '9th November, 1833' following it. In one other, more important respect the 'Epitaph' of 1834 lacks an element which, from all indications, the poet wished to associate with it: the Greek and Latin puns that appear in the last two manuscript versions. It is hard to understand why the poet would have expunged a feature that he had so painstakingly created, but in the absence of Coleridge's own manuscript for version 8 we cannot say whether or not he did. Fortunately, we are not limited to one ultimate received text and are free to explore the meanings of Coleridge's puns on his own initials.

The names that Coleridge made up by transliterating his initials into English or Greek are only some of the extraordinary variety of names that he employed both within his literary life and outside it. It was common in his time for authors to use *noms de plume*, but Coleridge invested his with symbolic meaning and deployed them with uncommon zest— Nicias Erythraeus, Nehemiah Higginbottom, Laberius, Satyrane, Silas Tomkyn Comberbache, among others.[47] There are also those nameless alter egos, the person from Porlock in the prose preface to 'Kubla Khan' and the 'friend' whose 'very judicious letter' figures so prominently in Chapter 13 of the *Biographia* (*BL* i. 300–4). For Coleridge such fictions obviously embodied aspects of himself, and this is nowhere so true as when their names were made up of variations on his own initials. The simplest of these are English phonetic transcriptions, such as ESTEESI after 'A Christmas Carol' in the *Annual Anthology* for 1799,[48] or variations like SIESTI after 'To Two Sisters' in *The Courier* for 10 December 1807 (*CPW* i. 410 n.). A step beyond these is transliteration into Greek of the kind displayed by the seal Coleridge had cut for sealing letters at Malta.[49] The Greek letters were also used as the signature for the 'Dejection' ode as it first appeared in the *Morning Post* for 4 April 1802 (*CPW* i. 369 n.) and for a number of other poems, including the original publications of 'A Christmas Carol' (*CM* i. 93 n.), 'The Keepsake' (*CPW* i. 345n.), and 'The Day-Dream' (*CPW* i. 387 n.). We can see in one sense what Coleridge meant when he wrote in the 'advertisement'

[46] *Letters of Samuel Taylor Coleridge* (2 vols., London: William Heinemann, 1895), ii. 769 n.
[47] On some of Coleridge's pseudonymns, see Carl Woodring, *Politics in the Poetry of Coleridge* (Madison, Wis.: University of Wisconsin Press, 1961), 229–30.
[48] See *CPW* i. 340 n., *CM* i. 93 and n.
[49] See *CL* ii. 1160 n. The seal was inscribed with the letters and S. T. C.; it is reproduced on the title pages of *CC*.

to the fifth version of his 'Epitaph' that he was 'better known' by his initials than by his name. Yet there is another sense to 'better known', in that the reader is imagined as gaining a better knowledge of the author from the persona formed by his initials than from his ordinary name.

There is ample evidence for Coleridge's dislike of his '*wobbling* name, Samuel'.[50] His true self, or aspects of it, could be expressed in the names he invented, the most important of which were those which demonstrated his ability to create a new identity from the nominal materials that circumstances had provided. Jerome C. Christensen has aptly commented on the nameless correspondent of the *Biographia*:

> Coleridge's correspondent is a man of letters in the conventional sense: the man of letters is strictly a man of letters because he has no existence outside of the text that Coleridge attributes to him, no life outside the text, in which these words appear.[51]

Such a conception is carried even further in Coleridge's 'ESTEESI' or its Greek transliteration. Here it is the poet rather than a fictitious correspondent, who is both literally and figuratively a man of letters, a being with a purely textual existence. Even this transformation is, however, not enough for Coleridge. By demonstrating an arcane meaning enacted by the letters, he can enable his true self—that is, the self he has created—to be better-known than his wobbling name.

One of Coleridge's earliest explanations of this strategy is found in a letter to William Sotheby dated 10 September 1802:

> ῍Εστησε signifies—*He hath stood*—which in these times of apostasy from the principles of Freedom, or of Religion in this country, & from both by the same persons in France, is no unmeaning Signature, if subscribed with humility, & in the remembrance of, Let him that stands take heed lest he fall—. However, it is in truth nothing more than S. T. C. written in Greek. *Es tee see* [.]
>
> (*CL* ii. 867 n.)

Scholars have pointed out that here and in several similar contexts Coleridge evidently attempted to force the Greek meaning he desired at the expense of correctness.[52] That this was indeed the case is strongly suggested by lines he wrote about himself in 'A Character':

> Thus, his own whim his only bribe,
> Our Bard pursued his old A. B. C.

---

[50] See Whalley in *CM* i. 93n, 2:; *CL* ii. 1126.

[51] *Coleridge's Blessed Machine of Language* (Ithaca, NY: Cornell University Press, 1981), 169.

[52] See Griggs in *CL* ii. 867 n. and Cecil C. Seronsy, 'Marginalia by Coleridge in Three Copies of His Published Works', *Studies in Philology*, 51 (1954), 471 n.

Contented if he could subscribe
In fullest sense his ῎Εστησε;
('Tis Punic Greek for 'he hath stood!')
(*CPW* i. 453)

Presumably, 'Punic Greek' or punning Greek permits a certain latit-
ude, in this case allowing Coleridge's Greek cognomen to echo the
meaning of Martin Luther's 'Here I stand'.[53] In a letter to William
Godwin dated 30 December 1818, the meaning is rendered as '*He hath
stood firm*' (*CL* iv. 1167). Such linguistic play first appears in conjunc-
tion with the 'Epitaph' in the letter to J. H. Green containing version 4;
with version 6 it appears both horizontally and vertically in the poem
itself; and in version 7 it is, as Whalley puts it, 'set at the end of the poem
like a formal lapidary inscription', underscoring the link between epitaph and inscription discussed at the beginning of this chapter:

ἔστη. κεῖται. ἀναστήσει.
Stetit: restat: resurget.

ΕΣΤΗΣΕ[54]

Thus a theme that was so prominent more than a quarter of a century
before, in 'To William Wordsworth', returns in Coleridge's 'Epitaph'
with the assurance of one who knows himself to have stood and who believes that he will rise again. One might say that the elements of
Coleridge's self-invented name have replaced the personifications of
previous later poems, and that it is now they who enact a drama of suffering, death, and resurrection, bringing to an appropriate close the
period of Coleridge's later poetry.

---

[53] See note by Whalley in *CM* i. 93 n., and Fulford, *Coleridge's Figurative Language*, 29.

[54] *CL* vi. 973; *CM* ii. 905 n. Whalley translates: 'He hath stood; he lies at rest; he will rise
again | Here lies one who hath stood, awaits, will rise again.' 'ἔστη' shows that Coleridge re-
cognized the correct Greek aorist form for 'he stood'. For further discussion of the
significance of the Greek pun, see Fulford, *Coleridge's Figurative Language* (Basingstoke and
London, 1991), 158.

SUPPLEMENTARY NOTE
THE ABRAHAM WIVELL PORTRAIT

On 6 November 1833 Coleridge wrote to the engraver and publisher E. F. Finden concerning drawings of himself that might be used for a portrait engraving (*CL* vi. 973–4). This was, as E. L. Griggs notes, in response to a communication from Charles Lamb saying, 'Mr. Finden, an artist of some celebrity, is desirous of publishing an Engraving of you . . . can you lend him your head?' Coleridge informed Finden that there were two drawings of himself at Highgate. His own favorite was that 'taken off hand, some 15 years ago, by Mr. Lesly' [Charles Leslie]. The other was the recent (1833) pencil drawing by J. Kayser. Coleridge had addressed a poem to the artist, but he evidently did not like the portrait, 'with such unhappy Density of the Nose & ideotic Drooping of the Lip, with a certain pervading *Wooden[n]ess* of the whole Countenance'. Finden was informed that 'Mr S. T. C. will be found at home, "The Grove, Highgate" any day, *after 1* o'clock.'

E. F. Finden produced, as Griggs notes, a portrait engraving for the second edition of *Table Talk*. The original was neither by Leslie nor by Kayser, but a different portrait by Thomas Phillips. However, Finden had another connection with Coleridge portraiture. Like a number of other prosperous engravers, Finden was also a publisher specializing in illustrated books. In 1834 he brought out *Finden's Illustrations of the Life and Works of Lord Byron*, published by John Murray. Volume 3 (unpaginated) includes a portrait of Coleridge (reproduced as the frontispiece to this book). The artist was Abraham Wivell (1786–1849),[1] known for his sketches of the Cato Street conspirators and of figures involved in the trial of Queen Caroline; the engraver was W. Wagstaff. Although the date of the original portrait (untraced) is not known, it shows Coleridge late in life, his hair snow-white. Proofs of an illustration to be published in 1834 would very likely have been ready by late 1833, and Coleridge no doubt received complimentary copies. Among the books formerly owned by Coleridge that were disposed of in the James Gillman sale was 'Illustrations to Byron's Works, *engraver's proofs before letters*, in a portfolio'.[2]

[1] See Samuel Redgrave, *A Dictionary of Artists of the English School* (London, rev. edn., 1890) s.v.

[2] *Catalogue of a Valuable Collection of Books, Including the Library of James Gillman, Esq.,*

In a letter conjectured by E. L. Griggs to have been written in November 1833, Coleridge asked Eliza Aders, 'Is one of Wyville's [*sic*] Proofs of my face worth Mr Aders' acceptance?' (*CL* vi. 969) and went on to say that he had written a transcription from Ovid under another such proof and sent it to Henry Nelson Coleridge. (See above, p. 120). Griggs notes two engraved portraits of Coleridge after Wivell: one engraved by T. B. Welch for the frontispiece of *The Works of Samuel Taylor Coleridge, Prose and Verse* (Philadelphia, 1840), the second engraved by J. F. E. Proudhomme for the frontispiece of the first volume of W. G. T. Shedd's edition of *The Complete Works of Samuel Taylor Coleridge* (1853).[3] It seems unlikely, however, that proofs of a portrait engraving not to be published until years after Coleridge's death were in existence in 1833. A much likelier candidate is one published in 1834, at least one proof of which we know Coleridge owned. This engraving deserves to be better known, and it is to be hoped that the original drawing will one day be discovered.

Deceased (removed from Highgate . . .) (London: Henry Southgate & Co., Mar. 30, Mar. 31, & Apr. 1, 1843), 29 (no. 757).

[3] See *CL* vi. 969 n.; and Richard Walker, *Regency Portraits* (2 vols., London: National Portrait Gallery, 1985), i. 122.

BIBLIOGRAPHY

MANUSCRIPT SOURCES

British Library: Add. Mss. 34225, 47499, 47514, 47515, 47516, 47517, 47523, 47524, 47526, 47547. Book classmarks: C. 44. g. 1, C. 43. a. 1.
Cornell University Wordsworth Collection, nos. 2620, 2623, 3186.
Dove Cottage Library, Grasmere: Mss. 14/7, 41.
Harry Ransom Humanities Research Center, University of Texas at Austin: Sara Coleridge's Album.
Henry E. Huntington Library: HM 360, HM 8195, HM 12122.
New York Public Library, Berg Collection: 'Berg Notebook', 'Clasped Vellum Notebook', 'Notebook Q'.
Pierpont Morgan Library: MA 1581 (Coleridge 13), book no. 49359.

PRINTED SOURCES

ABRAMS, M. H. *Natural Supernaturalism*: *Tradition and Revolution in Romantic Literature* (New York, 1971).
The Amulet for 1828.
The Annual Register for 1825.
The Annual Register for 1827.
ANON., *Eternal Punishment Proved to Be Not Suffering, but Privation* (London, 1817).
The Anti-Jacobin, 20 Nov. 1797.
BACHELARD, GASTON, *The Poetics of Space*, trans. Marie Jolas (New York, 1964).
BARTH, J. ROBERT, SJ, 'Coleridge's Constancy to His Ideal Object', *The Wordsworth Circle*, 14 (1983), 76–80.
BARTAS, GUILLAUME DE SALLUSTE, seigneur du, *The Divine Weeks and Works of Guillaume De Saluste Sieur Du Bartas*, trans. Josua Sylvester, ed. Susan Snyder (2 vols., Oxford, 1979), i.
BATE, WALTER JACKSON, *Coleridge* (London, 1969 [1968]).
BEER, JOHN, *Coleridge the Visionary* (London, 1959).
—— , *Coleridge's Poetic Intelligence* (London, 1970).
—— (ed.), *Coleridge's Variety: Bicentenary Studies* (Pittsburgh, 1975).
BENNETT, SHELLEY M., *Thomas Stothard: The Mechanisms of Art Patronage in England circa 1800* (Columbia, Mo., 1988).
The Bijou for 1828.
Blackwood's Edinburgh Magazine, 31 (1832).

BLAKE, WILLIAM, *The Complete Poetry and Prose of William Blake*, ed. David V. Erdman (Garden City, New York, rev. edn., 1982).

BLOOM, HAROLD, *Introduction to Samuel Taylor Coleridge: Modern Critical Views* (New York, 1986).

BOCCACCIO, GIOVANNI, *The Decameron*, trans. W. K. Kelley (London, 1855).

BOULGER, JAMES D., *Coleridge As Religious Thinker* (New Haven, 1961).

——, *The Calvinist Temper in English Poetry* (The Hague, 1981).

BOUSLOG, CHARLES, 'The Symbol of the Sod-Seat in Coleridge', *PMLA* 60 (1945), 802–10.

BROWNE, SIR THOMAS, *Religio Medici* (4th edn., London, 1656).

BROWNELL, MORRIS R., *Alexander Pope & the Arts of Georgian England* (Oxford, 1978).

BURWICK, FREDERICK, 'Coleridge's "Limbo" and "Ne Plus Ultra": The Multeity of Intertextuality', *Romanticism Past and Present*, 9 (1985), 73–95.

CARLYLE, THOMAS, *The Life of John Sterling* (London, 1897).

CHRISTENSEN JEROME, *Coleridge's Blessed Machine of Language* (Ithaca, NY, 1981).

CHRISTIE, MANSON, and WOODS, *The Larger Blake-Varley Sketchbook* (London, 21 July 1989).

COBURN, KATHLEEN, 'Reflections in a Coleridge Mirror: Some Images in His Poems', in *From Sensibility to Romanticism*, ed. Frederick Hilles and Harold Bloom (New York, 1965), 415–37.

——, *Experience into Thought: Perspectives in the Coleridge Notebooks* (Toronto, 1979).

COLERIDGE, ARTHUR DUKE, *Reminiscences*, ed. J. A. Fuller-Maitland (London, 1921).

COLERIDGE, SAMUEL TAYLOR, *Aids to Reflection* [*CC* ix], ed. John Beer (Princeton, NJ, 1993).

——, *Biographia Literaria*, ed. J. Shawcross, 2 vols. (Oxford, rev. edn. 1954).

——, *Biographia Literaria* [*CC* vii], ed. James Engell and W. Jackson Bate (2 vols., Princeton, NJ, 1983).

——, *Christabel; Kubla Khan, A Vision; The Pains of Sleep* (London, 1817).

——, *Coleridge's Verse; A Selection*, ed. William Empson and David Pirie (London, 1972).

——, *Collected Letters of Samuel Taylor Coleridge*, ed. Earl Leslie Griggs, 6 vols. (Oxford, 1956–71).

——, *Complete Poetical Works of Samuel Taylor Coleridge*, ed. Ernest Hartley Coleridge, 2 vols. (Oxford, 1912).

——, *Complete Works of Samuel Taylor Coleridge*, ed. W. G. T. Shedd (7 vols., New York, 1884), v.

——, *Confessions of an Inquiring Spirit*, ed. H. St. J. Hart BD (London, 1956).

——, *The Friend* [*CC* iv.], ed. Barbara E. Rooke, 2 vols. (Princeton, NJ, 1969).

——, *Hints Towards the Formation of a More Comprehensive Theory of Life*, ed. Seth B. Watson (London, 1848).

COLERIDGE, SAMUEL TAYLOR, *Lay Sermons* [*CC* vi], ed. R. J. White (Princeton, NJ, 1972).

——, *Lectures 1795 On Politics and Religion* [*CC* i], ed. Lewis Patton and Peter Mann (Princeton, 1971).

——, *Lectures 1808–1819: On Literature* [*CC* v], ed. R. A. Foakes, 2 vols. (Princeton, NJ, 1987).

——, *Letters of Samuel Taylor Coleridge*, ed. Ernest Hartley Coleridge (2 vols., London, 1895), ii.

——, *The Literary Remains of Samuel Taylor Coleridge*, ed. Henry Nelson Coleridge (4 vols., London, 1836), i.

——, *Marginalia*, ed. George Whalley and H. J. Jackson (3 vols., Princeton, 1980–92).*CC* xii.

——, *The Notebooks of Samuel Taylor Coleridge*, ed. Kathleen Coburn *et al.*, 5 vols. (Princeton, 1957–).

——, *On the Constitution of the Church and State* [*CC* x], ed. John Colmer (Princeton, NJ, 1976).

——, *The Philosophical Lectures of Samuel Taylor Coleridge*, ed. Kathleen Coburn (New York, 1949).

——, *Poems*, ed. John Beer (rev. edn., London, 1993).

——, *The Poems of Samuel Taylor Coleridge*, ed. Sara Coleridge and Derwent Coleridge (London, 1852).

——, *The Poetical Works of Samuel Taylor Coleridge*, 3 vols. (London, 1828).

——, *The Poetical Works of Samuel Taylor Coleridge*, 3 vols. (London, 1829).

——, *The Poetical Works of Samuel Taylor Coleridge*, 3 vols. (London, 1834).

——, *The Poetical Works of Samuel Taylor Coleridge*, ed. James Dykes Campbell (London, 1893).

——, *Samuel Taylor Coleridge*, ed. H. J. Jackson (Oxford, 1985).

——, *Sibylline Leaves: A Collection of Poems* (London, 1817).

——, *Table Talk* [*CC* xiv], ed. Carl Woodring, 2 vols. (Princeton, NJ, 1990).

——, and SOUTHEY, ROBERT, *Omniana* (2 vols., London, 1812), ii.

COLMER, JOHN, 'Coleridge and the Life of Hope', *Studies in Romanticism*, 11 (1972), 332–41.

COOKE, MICHAEL, 'The Manipulation of Space in Coleridge's Poetry', in *New Perspectives on Coleridge and Wordsworth*, ed. Geoffrey Hartman (New York, 1972), 165–94.

DANTE ALIGHIERI, *La Divina Commedia di Dante Alighieri*, ed. Manifredi Porena (Bologna, 1994–5).

DONNE, JOHN, *The Poetical Works of John Donne* (Edinburgh, 1793).

——, *The Sermons of John Donne*, ed. George R. Potter and Evelyn M. Simpson (Berkeley and Los Angeles, 1962), i.

——, *The Poems of John Donne*, ed. Herbert J. C. Grierson (London, 1963 [1912]), i.

——, *John Donne: The Satires, Epigrams, and Verse Letters*, ed. W. Milgate (Oxford, 1967).

DORENKAMP, ANGELA G., 'Hope At Highgate: The Late Poetry of Coleridge', *The Barat Review*, 6 (1971), 59–66.

ELIOT, T. S., *Collected Poems 1909–62* (London, 1963).

EMERSON, RALPH WALDO, *English Traits* (London, 1856).

FLETCHER, ANGUS, ' "Positive Negation": Threshold, Sequence, and Person-ification in Coleridge', in *New Perspectives on Coleridge and Wordsworth*, ed. Geoffrey Hartman (New York, 1972), 133–64.

Friendship's Offering for 1834.

FULFORD, Tim. *Coleridge's Figurative Language* (Basingstoke and London, 1991).

——, 'Apocalyptic and Reactionary: Coleridge as Hermenutist', *Modern Language Review*, 87 (1992), 22–5.

——, 'Paradise Rewritten? Coleridge's *The Blossoming of the Solitary Date-Tree*', *The Wordsworth Circle*, 24 (1993), 83–5.

FULLER, THOMAS, *Abel Redevivus / or / The dead yet speaking* (London, 1652).

GIBBS, WARREN E., 'S. T. Coleridge's "The Knight's Tomb" and "Youth and Age" ', *Modern Language Review*, 28 (1933), 83–5.

GILCHRIST, ALEXANDER, *The Life of William Blake*, ed. Ruthven Todd (2nd edn., London, 1945).

GILL, STEPHEN, *William Wordsworth: A Life* (Oxford, 1989).

GRATTAN, COLLEY, *Beaten Paths; And Those Who Trod Them* (2 vols., London, 1862), i.

GRAVES, ROBERT PERCEVAL, *Life of Sir William Rowan Hamilton* (3 vols., London and Dublin, 1882), i.

GREW, NEHEMIAH, *Cosmologia Sacra* (London, 1701).

HAMILTON, PAUL, *Coleridge's Poetics* (Oxford, 1983).

HARTMAN, GEOFFREY, 'Inscriptions and Romantic Nature Poetry', *The Un-remarkable Wordsworth*, Theory and History of Literature Ser. 34 (Minnea-polis, 1987) 31–46.

HECKSHER, WILLIAM S., 'Shakespeare and the Visual Arts', *Research Opportun-ities in Renaissance Drama: The Report of the Modern Language Association Seminar*, ed. S. Schoenbaum, 13–14 (1970–1), 35–56.

HERBERT, GEORGE, *The Works of George Herbert*, ed. F. E. Hutchinson (Oxford, 1945 [1941]).

HILL, GEOFFREY, *The Lords of Limit: Essays on Literature and Ideas* (New York, 1984).

HODGSON, JOHN A., 'Coleridge, Puns, and "Donne's First Poem": The Limbo of Rhetoric and the Conception of Wit', *John Donne Journal*, 4 (1985), 181–200.

HORTON, RONALD A., 'Satyrane', *The Spenser Cyclopedia*, ed. A. C. Hamilton (Toronto, 1990).

HUNT, LEIGH, *Imagination and Fancy* (New York, 1845 [1844]).

——, *The Autobiography of Leigh Hunt*, ed. J. E. Morpurgo (London, 1948).

HUTCHINSON, SARA, *The Letters of Sara Hutchinson*, ed. Kathleen Coburn (London, 1954).

JACKSON, J. DE G. (ed.), *Coleridge: The Critical Heritage* (London, 1971).

JOHNSON, MARY LYNN, 'How Rare is a "Unique Annotated Copy" of Coleridge's *Sibylline Leaves?*' *Bulletin of the New York Public Library*, 76 (1975), 451–81.

KEATS, JOHN, *Letters of John Keats*, ed. Hyder Edward Rollins, 2 vols. (Cambridge, Mass., 1958).

The Keepsake for 1829.

The Keepsake for 1830.

KESSLER, EDWARD, *Coleridge's Metaphors of Being* (Princeton, NJ, 1979).

KNAPP, STEPHEN, *Personification and the Sublime: Milton to Coleridge* (Cambridge, Mass., 1985).

KNIGHT, WILLIAM, *Memorials of Coleorton* (Boston, 1897).

KORSHIN, PAUL, *Typologies in England: 1660–1820* (Princeton, NJ, 1982).

LAMB, CHARLES, *The Essays of Elia*, ed. Augustine Birrell (London, 1907).

LATTIMORE, RICHARD, *Themes in Greek and Latin Epigraphs* (Urbana, Ill., 1962).

LEFEBURE, MOLLY, *Samuel Taylor Coleridge: A Bondage of Opium* (London, 1974).

——, *The Bondage of Love* (London, 1986).

LESSING, GOTTHOLD EPHRAIM, *Sämmtliche Schriften*, 30 vols. (Berlin, 1796, 1784–94).

The Literary Souvenir for 1827.

The Literary Souvenir for 1828.

LOGAN, SISTER EUGENIA, *A Concordance to the Poetry of Coleridge* (Saint Mary-of-the Woods, Ind., 1940).

LOWES, JOHN LIVINGSTON, *The Road to Xanadu* (London, 1927).

LUTHER, SUSAN, 'The Lost Garden of Coleridge', *The Wordsworth Circle*, 22 (1992), 24–30.

McCUSICK, JAMES C., *Coleridge's Philosophy of Language* (New Haven, 1986).

——, ' "Living Words": Samuel Taylor Coleridge and the Genesis of the *OED*', *Modern Philology*, 90 (1992), 1–45.

McFARLAND, THOMAS, *Coleridge and the Pantheist Tradition* (Oxford, 1969).

——, *Romanticism and the Forms of Ruin: Wordsworth, Coleridge, and the Modalities of Fragmentation* (Princeton, NJ, 1981).

MAHONEY, JOHN L., ' "We Must Away": Tragedy and Imagination in Coleridge's Later Poems', *Coleridge, Keats, and the Imagination: Romanticism and Adam's Dream, Essays in Honor of Walter Jackson Bate*, ed. J. Robert Barth SJ and John L. Mahoney (Columbia, Mo., 1990).

MESMER, F. A., *Mesmerismus, oder System der Wechselwirkungen, Theorie, und Anwendung des thierischen Magnetismus . . .*, ed. K. C. Wolfart, 2 vols. (Berlin, 1814–15).

MILEUR, JEAN-PIERRE, *Vision and Revision: Coleridge's Art of Immanence* (Berkeley and Los Angeles, 1982).

NEWLYN, LUCY, *Coleridge, Wordsworth, and the Language of Allusion* (Oxford, 1986).

NYE, ERIC W., 'Coleridge and the Publishers: Twelve New Manuscripts', *Modern Philology*, 87 (1989), 51–71.

PALEY, MORTON D., ' "These Promised Years": Coleridge's "Religious Musings" and the Millenarianism of the 1790s', *Revolution and English Romanticism*, ed. Keith Hanley and Raman Selden (Hemel Hempstead, Hants., 1990), 49–66.

——, 'Coleridge's "Preternatural Agency" ', *European Romantic Review*, 1 (1991), 135–46.

——, 'Apocalypse and Millennium in the Poetry of Coleridge', *The Wordsworth Circle*, 23 (1992), 24–34.

——, 'Coleridge and the Apocalyptic Grotesque', *Coleridge's Visionary Languages*, ed. Tim Fulford and Morton D. Paley (Woodbridge, Suffolk, 1993), 15–25.

——, 'Coleridge and the Annuals', *Huntington Library Quarterly*, 57 (1994), 1–24.

PALGRAVE, FRANCIS TURNER (ed.), *The Golden Treasury* (Cambridge and London, 1861).

PARKER, REEVE, *Coleridge's Meditative Art* (Ithaca, NY, 1975).

PEELE, GEORGE, *The Life and Minor Works of George Peele*, ed. David H. Horne (New Haven, 1952).

PRICKETT, STEPHEN, *Coleridge and Wordsworth: The Poetry of Growth* (Cambridge, 1970).

Quarterly Review (52 [August and November 1834]).

RAJAN, TILOTTAMA, *Dark Interpreter: The Discourse of Romanticism* (Ithaca, NY, 1980).

——, *The Supplement of Reading* (Ithaca, NY, 1990).

——, 'Coleridge, Wordsworth, and the Textual Abject', *The Wordsworth Circle*, 24 (1993), 61–8.

REDGRAVE, SAMUEL, *A Dictionary of Artists of the English School* (rev. edn. London, 1890).

REIMAN, DONALD H. (ed.), *The Romantics Reviewed*, A, ii (New York, 1972).

RICHARDS, I. A., *Coleridge's Minor Poems: A Lecture . . . Delivered . . . at Montana State University on April 8, 1960* (Missoula, Mo., 1960).

RIDENOUR, GEORGE F., 'Source and Allusion in Some Poems of Coleridge', *Studies in Philology*, 60 (1963), 187–95.

ROBERTS, MICHAEL (ed.), *The Faber Book of Comic Verse* (London, 1942).

SANDFORD, MRS HENRY, *Thomas Poole and His Friends*, 2 vols. (London, 1888).

SCHAFFER, E. S., *'Kubla Khan' and The Fall of Jerusalem: The Mythological School in Biblical Criticism and Secular Literature 1770–1880* (Cambridge, 1975).

SCHULZ, MAX, *The Poetic Voices of Coleridge* (Detroit, 1963).

SERONSY, CECIL C., 'Marginalia by Coleridge in Three Copies of His Published Works', *Studies in Philology*, 51 (1954), 470–81.

SHAKESPEARE, WILLIAM, *Twelfth Night*, ed. E. J. M. Lothian and T. W. Craik (London, 1975).

—— *The Tempest*, ed. Frank Kermode (Cambridge, Mass., 1958 [1954]).

SHELLEY, PERCY BYSSHE, *Shelley's Poetry and Prose*, ed. Donald H. Reiman and Sharon B. Powers (New York, 1977).

SMITH, CHARLOTTE, *Elegiac Sonnets* (7th edn., London, 1795).

SOUTHEY, ROBERT, *Poems* (Bristol and London, 1797 [Dec. 1796]).

SOUTHGATE, HENRY, & CO., *Catalogue of a Valuable Collection of Books, Including the Library of James Gillman, Esq., Deceased (removed from Highgate . . .)* (London, Mar. 30, Mar. 31, & Apr. 1, 1843).

STALLKNECHT, NEWTON P., *Strange Seas of Thought* (2nd edn. Bloomington, Ind., 1962).

STEVENS, WALLACE, 'The Figure of the Youth As a Virile Poet', *The Necessary Angel: Essays on Reality and the Imagination* (London, 1951).

TACITUS, CORNELIUS, *The Complete Works of Tacitus*, trans. Alfred John Church and William Jackson Brodribb (New York, 1942).

TENNEMAN, W. G., *Geshichte der Philosphie* (12 vols., Leipzig, 1798–1819).

WALKER, RICHARD, *Regency Portraits* (2 vols., London, 1985).

WARRINGTON, BERNARD, 'William Pickering, His Authors and Interests: A Publisher and the Literary Scene in the Early Nineteenth Century', *Bulletin of the John Rylands Library of the University of Manchester*, 69 (1987), 572–625.

WATSON, JEANIE, *Risking Enchantment: Coleridge's Symbolic World of Faery* (Lincoln, Nebr., 1990).

WATSON, LUCY, E. [neé Gillman], *Coleridge At Highgate* (London, 1925).

WATTS, ALFRED ALARIC, *Alaric Watts: A Narrative of His Life* (2 vols., London, 1884).

WELLS, CAROLYN (ed.), *A Nonsense Anthology* (New York, 1902).

WHALLEY, GEORGE, *Coleridge and Sara Hutchinson* (London, 1955).

——, 'Portrait of a Bibliophile VII: Samuel Taylor Coleridge', *The Book Collector*, n. v. (Autumn 1961), 275–90.

——, 'Coleridge's Poetical Canon: Selection and Arrangement', *A Review of English Literature*, 7 (1966), 9–23.

——, ' "Late Autumn's Amaranth": Coleridge's Late Poems', *Transactions of the Royal Society of Canada*, 4th ser., 2 (1964), 159–79.

——, 'The Harvest on the Ground', *University of Toronto Quarterly*, 38 (1969), 248–76.

WILLEY, BASIL, *Samuel Taylor Coleridge* (London, 1972).

WOODRING, CARL, *Politics in the Poetry of Coleridge* (Madison, Wis., 1961).

WOOLF, DERRICK, 'Sara Coleridge's Marginalia', *The Coleridge Bulletin*, n.s. no. 2 (Autumn 1993), 5–14.

WORDSWORTH, JONATHAN, 'Some Unpublished Coleridge Marginalia', *Times Literary Supplement*, 58 (14 June 1957), 369.

WORDSWORTH, WILLIAM, *Poetical Works*, ed. Ernest. de Selincourt (5 vols., Oxford, 1947), iv.

——, *The Prelude or Growth of a Poet's Mind*, ed. Ernest De Selincourt, rev. Helen Darbishire (2nd edn., Oxford, 1959).

——, *The Prelude 1799, 1805, 1850*, ed. Jonathan Wordsworth, M. H. Abrams, and Stephen Gill (New York, 1979).

——, *Poems in Two Volumes*, ed. Jared Curtis (Ithaca, NY, 1983).

——, *The Prose Works of William Wordsworth*, ed. W. J. B. Owen and Jane Worthington Smyser (3 vols., Oxford, 1974).

——, *William Wordsworth*, ed. Stephen Gill (Oxford, 1990 [1984]).

—— and COLERIDGE, SAMUEL TAYLOR, *Lyrical Ballads 1798*, ed. W. J. B. Owen (2nd edn., London, 1980).

——, and WORDSWORTH, DOROTHY, *The Letters of William and Dorothy Wordsworth*, ed. Ernest de Selincourt, rev. Mary Moorman, ii. *The Middle Years*, Pt. 1: 1806–11 (2nd edn., Oxford, 1969).

—— and WORDSWORTH, DOROTHY, *The Letters of William and Dorothy Wordsworth*, ed. Ernest de Selincourt, rev. Mary Moorman and Alan G. Hill, iii. *The Middle Years*, Pt. 2: 1812–20 (2nd edn., Oxford, 1969).

WRIGHT, HERBERT G., *Boccaccio in England from Chaucer to Tennyson* (London, 1957).

INDEX